THE OFFICI

LIVERPOOL

FOOTBALL CLUB

ANNUAL

CONTENTS

Written & compiled
by Tony Lynch

Designed by Stuart Perry

All facts believed correct at the
time of going to press

Published by Grandreams Ltd
435-437 Edgware Road
Little Venice
London W2 1TH

Printed in Belgium

MATCH-BY-MATCH

PART ONE

By August 1996 Liverpool FC, England's most successful football club, had spent the previous six seasons trying to regain former glories.

Since winning the League Championship in 1989-90, only two other major trophies had found their way into the Anfield trophy cabinet. They were the FA Cup, following Liverpool's 2-0 defeat of Sunderland in the 1992 final, and the Coca-Cola Cup in 1995 in which the Reds defeated Bolton Wanderers 2-1 at Wembley.

In 1995-96 the Reds had finished third in the Premiership table and were runners-up to Manchester United in the FA Cup. This was the match in which United completed the 'double'.

All-in-all that's not a bad record over seven seasons. Indeed, it's a record that many clubs would be proud of. But at Anfield they expect more. Having been brought up on a diet of truly spectacular success, Liverpool's fans demand only the very best from their team!

Each and every member of the Liverpool squad knew what was expected in 1996-97...

LIVERPOOL'S SQUAD NUMBER	
(At the start of the 1996-97 season)	
1	David James
2	Rob Jones
3	John Scales
4	Jason McAteer
5	Mark Wright
6	Phil Babb
7	Steve McManaman
8	Stan Collymore
9	Robbie Fowler
10	John Barnes
11	Jamie Redknapp
12	Steve Harkness
13	Tony Warner
14	Neil Ruddock
15	Patrik Berger
16	Michael Thomas
17	-
18	Phil Charnock
19	Mark Kennedy
20	Stig Inge Bjornebye
21	Dominic Matteo
22	-
23	Jamie Carragher
24	Lee Jones
25	David Thompson

MIDDLESBROUGH 3   LIVERPOOL 3

Premier League - 17 August 1996 - Att: 30,039

Liverpool's Premier League campaign got under way in the north-east with a visit to Middlesbrough's superb Riverside Stadium.

'Pool, playing for the first time in their new ecru shirts, went ahead after just four minutes when Stig Bjornebye squeezed between two 'Boro defender to fire home his first ever goal for Liverpool.

Then came a hotly-disputed penalty – in the 26th minute – which Ravanelli hammered home from the spot to level the score. John Barnes was the next name on the score-sheet, after expertly chesting the ball down and sliding it home in the 29th minute. By half time, Ravanelli had pounced again to level the scores again, following a defensive mix-up.

In the 65th minute Robbie Fowler put Liverpool ahead yet again after driving home a Stig Bjornebye cross. But it was Ravanelli's persistence which eventually saved the day for Middlesbrough. With nine minutes left to play he scored the last goal of the game and completed his hat-trick, by stabbing the ball past David James.

On the whole Liverpool had looked the better team and were disappointed not to bring all three points back to Anfield.

LIVERPOOL: *James; Wright, Matteo, Babb, McAteer, Thomas, McManaman, Barnes, Bjornebye, Collymore, Fowler*
Scorers: Bjornebye 4, Barnes 29, Fowler 65
Subs not used: Warner, Jones L, Ruddock, Thompson, Carragher

LIVERPOOL 2 ARSENAL 0

Premier League - 19 August 1996 - Att: 38,103

Arsenal came to Anfield for the Reds' first home encounter of the 1996-97 season. It was a tough game with honours even until well into the second half. The deadlock was finally broken in the 68th minute when Steve McManaman controlled an excellent John Barnes pass before firing in a shot which deflected off Steve Bould and into the net.

Six minutes later Super Steve was on target again. This time after he had set up John Barnes with a brilliant back-heeled pass. Barnsey drove the ball goalwards, it rebounded off David Seaman and was met by Macca who made no mistake.

The performance of skipper John Barnes impressed Roy Evans enough to say that he was worthy of a recall to the England squad. The Boss also declared himself happy with the way the Reds had started the season.

LIVERPOOL: *James; McAteer, Wright, Babb, Matteo, Bjornebye, Thomas, McManaman, Barnes, Collymore (Thompson 86), Fowler (Jones L 86)*
Scorer: McManaman 68, 74
Subs not used: Warner, Ruddock, Carragher

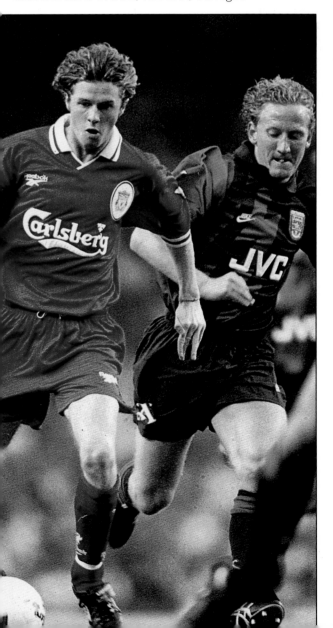

- *Above:* **Make 'em laugh! Sunderland keeper Tony Coton finds a novel way to deal with Robbie Fowler**
- *Left:* **Macca torments the Gunners**

LIVERPOOL 0 SUNDERLAND 0

Premier League - 24 August 1996 - Att: 40,503

Anfield's first 40,000+ crowd of the season turned out for the visit of Premier League newcomers Sunderland, managed by old Liverpool adversary Peter Reid. And Reidy's men put on a fine show to hold the Reds to a goal-less draw, with some spirited defending and an effective closing down policy. The visitors almost won the match, but thankfully Niall Quinn's shot was blocked en route to goal!

LIVERPOOL: *James; McAteer, Wright, Babb (Thompson 85), Matteo, Bjornebye, McManaman, Thomas, Collymore, Barnes, Fowler*
Subs not used: Warner, Ruddock, Jones L, Carragher

COVENTRY CITY 0   LIVERPOOL 1
Premier League – 4 September 1996 – Att: 23,021

Phil Babb was the hero of the hour for Liverpool in this hard fought victory over his old club. The Republic of Ireland defender won the match with his first ever goal for the Reds. It was scored from close in, in the 68th minute, from an inch-perfect cross by Jason McAteer following a free-kick on the right. The result marked Liverpool's first victory at Highfield Road in six years.

LIVERPOOL: *James; McAteer, Wright, Matteo, Babb, Bjornebye, Thomas, Barnes, McManaman, Collymore, Fowler*
Scorer: Babb 68
Subs not used: Warner, Redknapp, Ruddock, Berger, Jones L

LIVERPOOL 2   SOUTHAMPTON 1
Premier League – 7 September 1996 – Att: 39,189

Graeme Souness, former Liverpool star and manager, brought his new club to Anfield for the Reds' first home game in September.

Despite Liverpool's dominance, honours remained even for the first 38 minutes of the match. Then Stan Collymore stepped up to bag his first goal of the season. It came from a great pass by John Barnes. Stan mis-hit the ball, but Saints keeper Dave Beasant was already diving the wrong way and it finished in the back of the net.

Jim Magilton equalised for Southampton in the 57th minute, after Michael Thomas lost possession on the edge of the area. As the match wound towards the final whistle it was looking more and more like a draw. But in the last minute a crazy back-pass by Saints sub Neil Heaney allowed Steve McManaman a clear run at goal. Macca made no mistake and the three points lifted 'Pool to third place in the Premiership table.

LIVERPOOL: *James; McAteer, Wright (Ruddock 69), Matteo, Babb, Bjornebye, Thomas (Redknapp 77), Barnes, McManaman, Collymore (Berger 77), Fowler*
Scorers: Collymore 38, McManaman 89
Subs not used: Warner, Jones L

● *Top: **Stan Collymore, closely marked by Sky Blues' skipper Gary McAllister***
● *Below: **Stan gets shirty against the Saints!***

● *Patrik Berger scores at Filbert Street*

MYPA-47 0 LIVERPOOL 1

**European Cup-Winners' Cup 1st Rnd, 1st leg –
12 September 1996 – Att: 5,500**

1995-96 'double' winners Manchester United had
progressed as Premiership champs to the UEFA
Champions' League tournament. This meant that
Liverpool, as FA Cup runners-up, would be
England's representatives in the 1996-97 European
Cup-Winners' Cup competition.

The campaign got underway in the little town of
Anjalankoski, some 80 miles east of Helsinki, the
home of Finnish cup holders MyPa-47.

A team of part-timers, MyPa held out for an
hour before Stig Bjornebye blasted home a superbly
struck left-foot shot. It was Stig's first European goal,
scored on his European debut.

After that Liverpool relaxed and should have
increased the lead but Robbie Fowler and Michael
Thomas both hit the woodwork. In the end
Liverpool settled for a one-goal victory which stood
them in good stead for the return match at Anfield.

LIVERPOOL: *James; McAteer, Wright, Matteo, Babb,
Bjornebye, Thomas, Barnes, McManaman, Collymore,
Fowler*
Scorer: Bjornebye 61
*Subs not used: Warner, Ruddock, Redknapp, Berger,
Jones L*

LEICESTER CITY 0   LIVERPOOL 3

Premier League – 15 September 1996 – Att: 20,987

Three days after the trip to Norway, Liverpool were
back in Premiership action, at Filbert Street. In the
opening minute David James was forced to make a
fine save from Emile Heskey's point-blank shot.
After that the two teams seemed evenly-matched
and went in at half-time with the deadlock intact.

For the second half, Roy Evans substituted Stan
Collymore with Patrik Berger, a decision which
ultimately won the match for Liverpool. On 58
minutes the Czech Republic star took advantage of
a defensive error and shot the Reds ahead with a
brilliantly struck left-foot shot past Kasey Keller.
Three minutes later Liverpool were two-up when
Michael Thomas fired home from 20-yards after
connecting with a fine pass from Stig Bjornebye.

Patrik rounded off a great performance by
scoring Liverpool's third in the 77th minute after
being set-up by Jason McAteer and Robbie Fowler.

The result raised the Reds to top spot in the
Premier League table, but boss Roy Evans was
cautious about making any big predictions. 'There's a
long way to go yet,' he warned.

LIVERPOOL: *James; McAteer, Wright, Matteo, Babb,
Bjornebye, Thomas, Barnes, McManaman, Collymore
(Berger 46), Fowler*
Scorers: Berger 58, 77 Thomas 61
Subs not used: Warner, Ruddock, Redknapp, Jones L

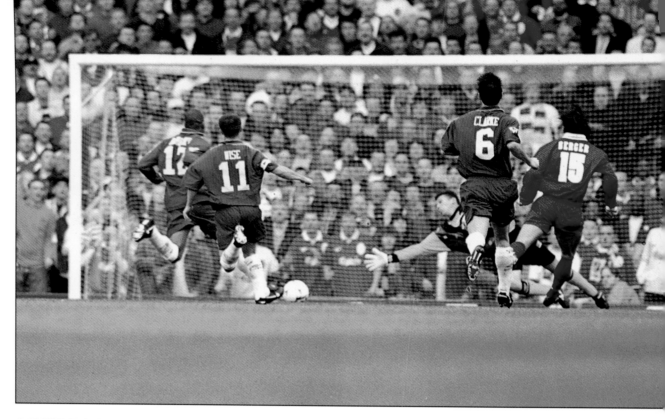

LIVERPOOL 5   CHELSEA 1

Premier League – 21 September 1996 – Att: 40,739

Ruud Gullit's Chelsea came to Anfield unbeaten in the League and with a reputation as one of the Premiership's classiest outfits. But the London Blues were totally outclassed by the Merseyside Reds.

The scoring began in the 14th minute when Robbie Fowler headed home a Stig Bjornebye cross from the left. Three minutes before half time Patrik Berger crowned his Anfield debut with the Reds' second goal, after latching onto a Dominic Matteo through-ball and rounding keeper Kevin Hitchcock.

On the stroke of half-time, Chelsea's Andy Myers inadvertently increased Liverpool's lead by heading into his own net. Another Chelsea error, this time by Dennis Wise, allowed Berger in for his second goal of the game on 48 minutes. Having collected the ball in midfield, Patrik took it all the way, to finish with a low shot past Hitchcock. Nine minutes later skipper John Barnes made it 5-0 with a well-struck volley which deflected off Franck Leboeuf before nestling in Chelsea's net.

The visitors were beaten but they did not give up. In the 86th minute that perseverance was rewarded with a consolation goal scored by Franck Leboeuf from the penalty spot. It was a brilliant result that consolidated the Reds' table-topping status.

LIVERPOOL: *James; McAteer, Wright, Matteo, Babb, Bjornebye, Thomas, Barnes, McManaman, Berger (Redknapp 78), Fowler*
Scorers: Fowler 14, Berger 42, 48, Myers (og) 45, Barnes 57
Subs not used: Warner, Ruddock, Collymore, Jones L

● *Above:* **Berger does it again this time against Chelsea**
● *Below:* **Patrick Berger opens the scoring against MyPa-47**

LIVERPOOL 3 MYPA-47 1

European Cup-Winners' Cup 1st Round, 2nd leg – 26 September 1996 – Att: 39,013

Liverpool's progress into the 2nd Round of the European Cup-Winners' Cup was assured with this convincing victory over the Finnish cup holders. The crowd, swelled by lower seat prices and the possibility of another devastating performance from Patrik Berger, was far bigger than anticipated.

Patrik did not disappoint. He continued his fine run of form by scoring the opening goal early in the game, after taking the ball off one Mypa defender and cheekily 'nutmegging' another. On the hour Stan Collymore opened his European account by putting the finishing touch to a great through-ball from John Barnes.

Four minutes later Keskitalo pulled one back for the visitors – his 20-yard shot gave David James no chance. In the 77th minute Captain Barnes completed the formalities with a close range goal after a wonderful solo run by Steve McManaman had set-up the chance.

LIVERPOOL: *James; McAteer, Wright (Scales 18), Matteo (Ruddock 79), Babb, Bjornebye, Thomas, Barnes, McManaman, Berger (Redknapp 79), Collymore*
Scorers: Berger 18, Collymore 60, Barnes 77
Subs not used: Warner, Jones L

WEST HAM 1 LIVERPOOL 2

Premier League – 29 September 1996 – Att: 25,064

Liverpool's winning ways continued with this Premiership clash at Upton Park. The opening goal came in the 3rd minute, from Stan Collymore at his devastating best. After collecting a fine pass from Jason McAteer, Stan ran with the ball from the halfway line before unleashing a low drive past keeper Ludek Miklosko.

But the EastEnders were in determined mood. They got back into the game after 15 minutes when Slaven Bilic headed home from a Mike Hughes corner. After that they turned up the pressure, but were unable to break through again.

The game's deciding moment came on 57 minutes when Michael Thomas scored after a magnificent passing move involving Jason McAteer and Steve McManaman.

LIVERPOOL: *James; McAteer, Scales (Ruddock 68), Matteo, Babb, Bjornebye, Thomas, Barnes, McManaman, Berger (Jones L 82), Collymore (Redknapp 19)*
Scorers: Collymore 3, Thomas 57
Subs not used: Warner, Kennedy

● ***Dominic Matteo deals with West Ham's Tony Cottee***

11

MANCHESTER UNITED 1
LIVERPOOL 0

Premier League – 12 October 1996 – Att: 55,128

Liverpool were dislodged from the Premiership top spot following their first league defeat of the season. Despite out-passing and out-playing United for most of the match, Liverpool could not find the necessary finishing power – and so lost out on the points. The only goal of the game came in the 23rd minute, from David Beckham's opportunist strike from 20-yards.

LIVERPOOL: *James; McAteer, Scales (Redknapp 80), Matteo, Babb, Bjornebye, Thomas, Barnes, McManaman, Berger Collymore*
Subs not used: Warner, Ruddock, Kennedy, Jones L

FC SION 1   LIVERPOOL 2

European Cup-Winners' Cup 2nd Round, 1st leg – 17 October 1996 – Att: 16,500

After going one-down due to a defensive error in the 11th minute, Liverpool took this game in hand to win with goals from Robbie Fowler and John Barnes. The winning margin might have been far wider but for the fine form of Sion keeper Stephan Lehmann.

LIVERPOOL: *James; McAteer, Scales, Matteo, Babb, Bjornebye, Thomas, Barnes, McManaman, Berger, Fowler (Redknapp 68)*
Scorers: Fowler 24, Barnes 60
Subs not used: Warner, Ruddock, Collymore, Kennedy

CHARLTON ATHLETIC 1
LIVERPOOL 1

Coca-Cola Cup 3rd Round – 23 October 1996 – Att: 15,000

A Robbie Fowler equaliser on 21 minutes was enough to earn a replay at Anfield in this hard-fought match. Charlton had gone ahead through David Whyte, who expertly lobbed David James in the 18th minute.

LIVERPOOL: *James; McAteer, Scales, Matteo, Babb, Bjornebye, Thomas, Barnes, McManaman, Berger, Fowler*
Scorer: Fowler 21
Subs not used: Ruddock, Redknapp, Collymore

● **John Barnes is challenged by Manchester United's Ronny Johnsen**

LIVERPOOL 2   DERBY COUNTY 1

Premier League – 27 October 1996 – Att: 39,515

Liverpool's first home encounter in five games brought Jim Smith's Derby County to Anfield. In the presence of England coach Glenn Hoddle, super striker Robbie Fowler pressed his claim for a regular international place by scoring both the Reds goals in the 2-1 victory.

The first came soon after the half-time interval when Red-Hot Robbie pounced on a rebounding ball from a shot by Patrik Berger. The second was a scorching header from a John Scales cross in the 51st minute. Ashley Ward pulled one back for Derby three minutes from time.

LIVERPOOL: James; McAteer, Scales, Matteo, Babb, Bjornebye, Thomas, Barnes, McManaman, Berger, Fowler
Scorer: Fowler 47, 51
Subs not used: Warner, Ruddock, Kennedy, Redknapp, Collymore

LIVERPOOL 6   FC SION 3

European Cup-Winners' Cup 2nd Round, 2nd leg – 31 October 1996 – Att: 38,514

Liverpool had to overcome another shaky start against Sion before powering a passage into the European Cup-Winners' Cup quarter-finals. By half-time the visitors were 2-1 ahead and the aggregate scores were level. Steve McManaman had supplied the Reds goal on 28 minutes, a low drive which beat Lehmann in the Sion goalmouth.

Things improved in the second period when Stig Bjornebye equalised from a free kick on 54 minutes. Then Sion scored a third which was cancelled out by a brilliant back-heeled strike from John Barnes.

From then on it was all Liverpool. Goal-hungry Robbie Fowler struck twice in the space of a minute, Patrik Berger scored in the 89th and Liverpool wrapped-up the tie with an 8-4 aggregate victory.

LIVERPOOL: James; McAteer, Scales (Redknapp 60), Matteo, Babb, Bjornebye, Thomas, Barnes, McManaman, Berger, Fowler
Scorers: McManaman 28, Bjornebye 54, Barnes 65, Fowler 70, 71, Berger 89
Subs not used: Warner, Ruddock, Collymore, Kennedy

● Left: **Red-hot Robbie Fowler heads home against Derby**
● Below: **John Barnes back-heels a goal against Sion**

MATCH-BY MATCH CONTINUES ON PAGE 25

DAVID JAMES

FACT FILE

Name: David Benjamin James
Birthdate: 1 August 1970
Birthplace: Welwyn Garden City
Height: 6' 5"
Weight: 14st 5lbs
Previous club: Watford
International: England Full, 'B',
Under-21

ROB JONES

FACT FILE

Name: Robert Marc Jones
Birthdate: 5 November 1971
Birthplace: Wrexham
Height: 5' 11"
Weight: 11st
Previous club: Crewe Alexandra
International: England Full,
Under-21, Youth, Wales Schools

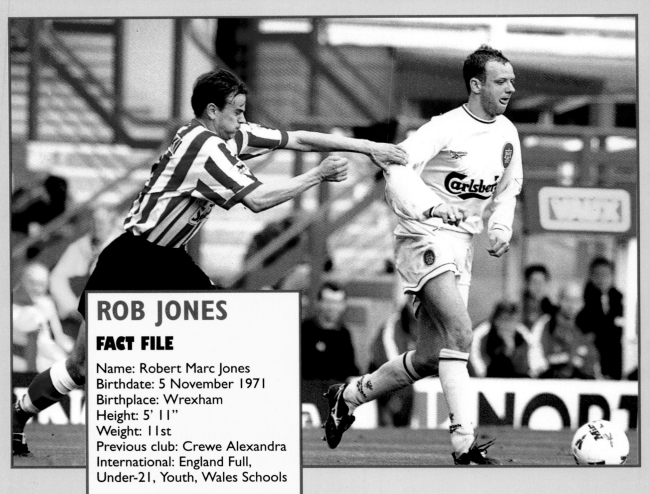

THE MAN IN RED BOOTS

John Charles Barnes (aka 'Digger') has always been a winner. In his days as a winger with Sudbury Court of the Middlesex Senior League, he was spotted by a sharp-eyed Watford supporter who alerted the Vicarage Road scouts to take a look at the gifted 17-year-old.

Watford's general manager Bertie Mee eventually got to take a look for himself and declared: 'How on earth could a player with such obvious qualities have been missed?'

John joined Second Division Watford in July 1981. He scored 13 goals in his first season – 1981-82 – and they were promoted to the top flight, under the guidance of future England manager Graham Taylor and flamboyant chairman Elton John.

A year later Watford finished as championship runners-up behind Liverpool. By then Barnsey had made the breakthrough at international level and would go on to accumulate 79 caps. In 1984 he played for Watford in the FA Cup final against Everton – and almost scored – but the Blues won the day 2-0.

Three weeks later John 'out-Brazil-ed' the Brazilians with a famous individual goal in England's first ever victory in Brazil. After receiving the ball wide of the left, he dribbled past four defenders before scoring.

When Graham Taylor left Watford in 1987 to take over the management of Aston Villa, the ambitious Barnes was next to go. He signed for Liverpool for £900,000.

The rest, as they say, is history. John went on to become one of Anfield best-loved players. He collected two League championship medals (1988, 1990), and one apiece in the FA and Coca-Cola cups (1989, 1995). He was twice voted Footballer of the Year by the Football Writers (1988, 1990),

and his fellow professionals made him their Player of the Year for 1988.

For the past two seasons he has worn the captain's armband for Liverpool and has revelled in his role of midfield general.

As the press persist in telling us, his days as a player may well be numbered now. But John Barnes has enjoyed a wonderful career with Liverpool – and he's bound to be equally successful in whatever he chooses to do after hanging up those famous red boots.

- *Above:* **The Skipper points the way**
- *Right:* **'Rushie' look on**

FACT FILE

Name: John Charles Barnes
Birthdate: 7 November 1963
Birthplace: Jamaica
Height: 5' 11"
Weight: 12st 7lbs
Previous club: Watford
International: England Full & Under-21

15

ANFIELD ACES

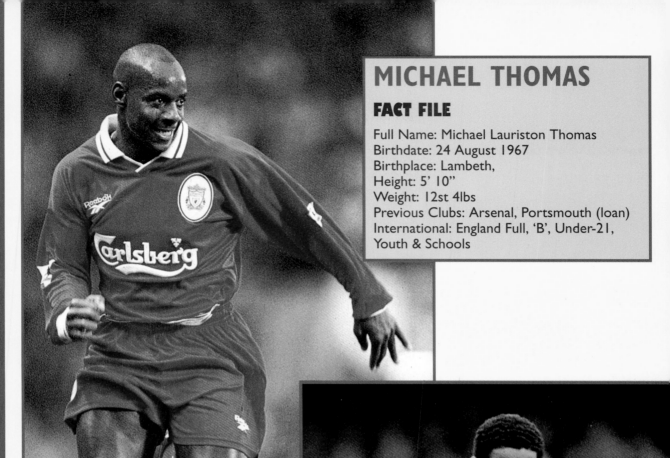

MICHAEL THOMAS

FACT FILE

Full Name: Michael Lauriston Thomas
Birthdate: 24 August 1967
Birthplace: Lambeth,
Height: 5' 10"
Weight: 12st 4lbs
Previous Clubs: Arsenal, Portsmouth (loan)
International: England Full, 'B', Under-21,
Youth & Schools

PHIL BABB

FACT FILE

Full Name: Philip Andrew Babb
Birthdate: 30 November 1970
Birthplace: Lambeth
Height: 6' 0"
Weight: 12st 3lbs
Previous clubs: Millwall, Bradford City,
Coventry City
International: Republic of Ireland 'B' & Full

BJORN FOR ANFIELD!

FACT FILE

Name: Bjorn Tore Kvarme
Birthdate: 17 July 1972
Birthplace: Trondheim
Previous club: Rosenborg

● *Above:* **Bjorn keeps Everton's Duncan Ferguson at bay**

As a soccer mad youngster growing up in Norway, Bjorn Kvarme avidly followed the exploits of his favourite club, Liverpool FC, and his hero was the ultra-talented Kenny Dalglish.

Now, at the age of 25, Bjorn is a hero to thousands of Liverpool fans who took to him straight away.

Suddenly there he was, a new face making his debut in the famous red strip, in a Premiership match against Aston Villa at Anfield. He gave such a polished and dogged defensive performance that he was voted Man of the Match.

Being out of contract in Norway, Bjorn had arrived on a free transfer in the wake of the Bosman ruling. Roy Evans had heard brilliant reports of the talented Norwegian – who had been a member of the Rosenborg side which had defeated AC Milan in the UEFA Champions League. And when the Liverpool boss saw him in action, he offered him a contract almost immediately.

An old friend of former Rosenborg star Stig Bjornebye, Bjorn quickly settled in with the rest of the Liverpool squad.

Now it seems as if he's always been an Anfielder!

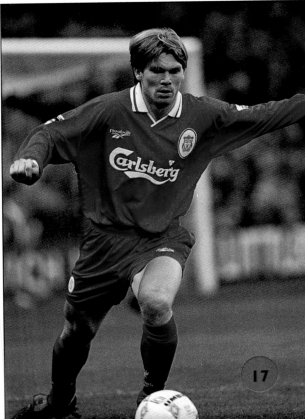

PATRIK BERGER

CLASS ACT

FACT FILE

Name: Patrik Berger
Birthdate: 10 November 1973
Previous clubs: Sparta Prague,
Borussia Dortmund
International: Czech Republic Full

To English eyes, midfield maestro Patrik Berger first came to prominence in that fabulous feast of football known as Euro '96. He had played twice at Anfield in Group C matches as the Czech Republic side made its way to the grand final.

It was Patrik who scored the first goal of that final, against Germany. It came in the 59th minute after Matthias Sammer was adjudged to have brought down Karel Poborsky in the box. Patrik took the penalty-kick and drove the ball past Andreas Kopke.

As everyone knows, the Germans equalised and went on to win the match in extra time. It was first time a major international final had been decided by the 'Golden Goal' ruling.

But that wasn't the end of the Czech Republic's association with England in 1996. Two of their top players would sign for English clubs after Euro '96. Karel Poborsky went to Manchester United from Slavia Prague. Patrik Berger joined Liverpool - after long drawn out negotiations with German Bundesliga champions Borussia Dortmund. The fee was finally agreed at £3.2 million and the Czech star returned to Anfield.

For Patrik the move was dream come true. As a youngster he had adopted Liverpool as his favourite football team, and recalled great games involving Kenny Dalglish and other famous Reds.

Patrik made an explosive start to his Liverpool career, and anyone thinking that wearing a hairband signified some sort of

weakness in a footballer, was made to think again!

After a substitute appearance for Stan Collymore late in the game against Southampton and two more matches sitting it out on the bench, Patrik was brought into the action for the second half of the Premiership match against Leicester at Filbert Street on 15 September 1996 – and he scored twice in Liverpool's 3-0 victory

In the next game he made his first start at Anfield, against Ruud Gullit's Chelsea – and he added two more goals to his account as the Reds thrashed the Blues 5-1.

Next came the European

● *Below: **Berger shoots against Leicester***

Cup-Winners' Cup tie against MyPa-47 at Anfield, he scored again as Liverpool marched on to the 2nd Round.

Five goals in two-and-a-half games, were enough to create another Anfield hero - and the 'BERGER15' shirt became a best seller in the club shop!

After such a wonderful start it was almost inevitable that an anti-climax would follow. Patrik would find himself in and out of the side as the season progressed. But he was far from worried by the situation. Everyone on the playing staff at Anfield knows and accepts that they are part of a squad system. Having a world class talent like Patrik Berger's on the sidelines simply underlines what a great squad it is!

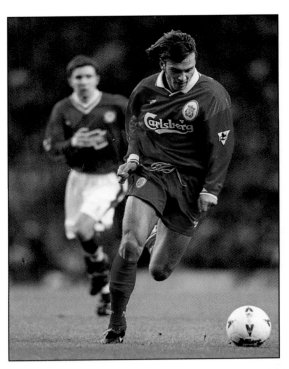

SUPERMAC!

MIDFIELD MAESTRO

FACT FILE

Name: Steven McManaman
Birthdate: 11 February 1972
Birthplace: Bootle
Height: 5' 11"
Weight: 10st 2lbs
Previous club: None
International: England Full,
Under-21 & Youth

To see the slim figure of Steve McManaman running at the opposition, his curly hair and red sleeves flapping in the breeze as he jinks past defenders – is one of English soccer's finest sights.

Liverpool and England team-mate Robbie Fowler reckons Steve is: 'One of the most exciting talents in the country. He can beat players for fun and it must be frightening for defenders to see him running at them – they've no idea which way he's going to go.'

Young Robbie is someone who definitely knows what he's talking about. Week-in, week-out he and his fellow forwards benefit from the sheer inventiveness of Macca's play.

Born in Bootle in February 1972, Steve attended Liverpool's School of Excellence as a schoolboy. He later became a trainee with the club and turned professional on 19 February 1990, just over a week after his 18th birthday.

Within two years he was a star performer, winning his first major medal when Liverpool beat Sunderland 2-0 in the 1992 FA Cup final.

A former England Youth player, he quickly broke into the international Under-21 ranks and even captained the side.

In 1995 he collected his second medal with Liverpool. This time he was the star of the show, scoring twice as the Reds beat Bolton Wanderers in the Cola-Cola Cup Final at Wembley.

Nowadays, Steve is a well-established favourite with the Anfield fans, and a regular member of Glenn Hoddle's England squad.

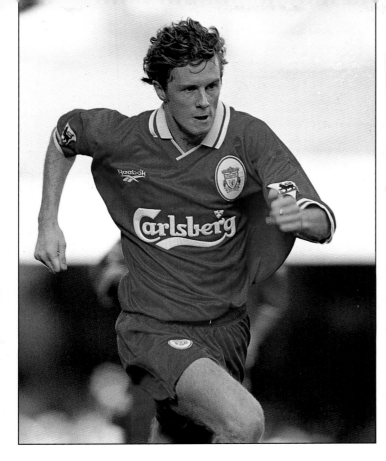

- *Opposite page top:* **Macca's pride after Liverpool's 1995 Coca-Cola Cup success. He holds the trophy and the Man of the Match award**
- *Opposite page below:* **Those trademark runs have been a feature of Macca's game, ever since he was given a 'roving' role by Roy Evans in 1994**
- *Right:* **In action against Coventry**
- *Below:* **Steve challenges Arsenal's Nigel Winterburn**

SUPERMAC!

NEIL RUDDOCK

FACT FILE

Name: Neil Ruddock
Birthdate: 9 May 1968
Birthplace: Wandsworth
Height: 6' 2"
Weight: 12st
Previous clubs: Millwall (twice),
Tottenham Hotspur (twice),
Southampton
International: England Full,
Youth, 'B' & Under-21

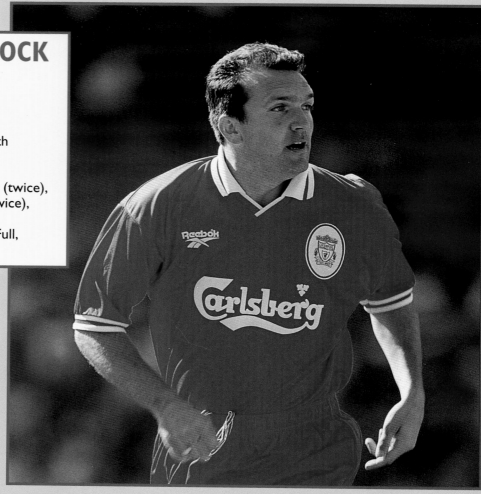

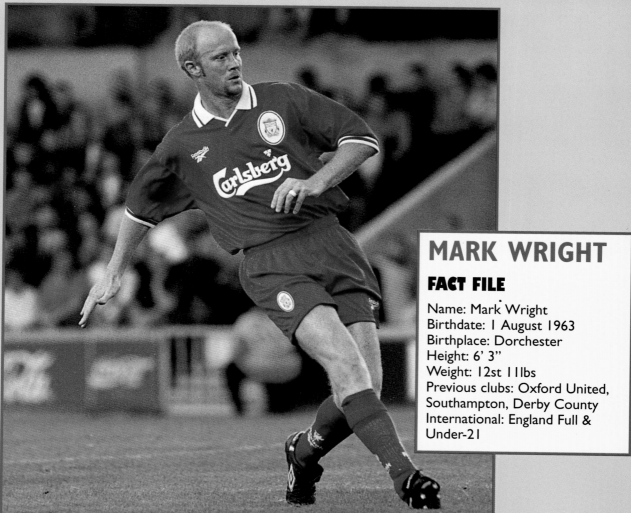

MARK WRIGHT

FACT FILE

Name: Mark Wright
Birthdate: 1 August 1963
Birthplace: Dorchester
Height: 6' 3"
Weight: 12st 11lbs
Previous clubs: Oxford United,
Southampton, Derby County
International: England Full &
Under-21

EVERYONE'S GLAD THAT STIG STUCK AROUND

Stig-Inge Bjornebye, Liverpool's Norwegian international defender, almost left Anfield at the start of the 1996-97 season. But he thought long and hard about the proposition before deciding to stay on.

Everyone at the club was delighted that he did, especially after the opening game of the Premiership campaign against Middlesbrough at the Riverside Stadium. This was Stig's comeback match after injury had ruled him out for much of the previous campaign – and that goal was his first ever for the club!

Five game later, he did it again. This time in the 61st minute of Liverpool's European Cup-Winners' Cup 1st Round away leg against MyPa-47 in Finland. It was the only goal of the game.

After that Stig's attacking forays became a regular feature of Liverpool's season. And he proved time and again that he is one of the club's most consistent performers.

- *Left:* **A heading duel against 'Boro**
- *Below:* **Stig-Inge Bjornebye – arguably Liverpool's most consistent performer in 1996-97**

FACT FILE

Name: Stig-Inge Bjornebye
Birthdate: 16 December 1969
Birthplace: Elvcrum
Previous club: Rosenborg
International: Norway Full

JASON McATEER
RED RIGHT THROUGH

Jason McAteer is another Liverpool star who supported the Reds as a lad. He is a Merseysider, born in Birkenhead in June 1971. But his playing career took him a little further afield, to Burnden Park, home of Bolton Wanderers who snapped him up from non-league Marine in 1992.

With Bolton he quickly developed into one of the best central midfield prospects in the country. And it was his performance against Liverpool in the 1995 Coca-Cola Cup final that finally persuaded Roy Evans it was time the young Merseysider came home – he signed him for £4.5 million in September 1995.

Jason adapted quickly to the Anfield scheme of things. And Roy Evans shrewdly converted him into a right-sided attacking wing-back – a ploy that has met with great success ever since. Many Liverpool goals have resulted from Jason's tireless runs and pinpoint crosses.

FACT FILE

Name: Jason Wynn McAteer
Birthdate: 18 June 1971
Birthplace: Birkenhead
Height: 5' 9"
Weight: 11st 5lbs
Previous club: Bolton Wanderers
International: Republic of Ireland Full & 'B'

BLACKBURN ROVERS 3
LIVERPOOL 0

Premier League – 3 November 1996 – Att: 29,598

Troubled Blackburn, without a manager and bottom of the table, chose this match to turn in the kind of performance that everyone knew they were capable of. Liverpool, who were caught in possession to often, could find no answer to two early goals – scored by Chris Sutton (a penalty) and Jason Wilcox. Early in the second half Sutton's second goal sealed the match in Rovers' favour.

It was Blackburn's first Premiership win of the season, and Liverpool's second defeat. Roy Evans was not pleased: 'We played badly,' he said. 'Blackburn fought hard and deserved to win.'

LIVERPOOL: *James; McAteer, Wright, Matteo, Babb, Bjornebye (Redknapp 33), Thomas, Barnes, McManaman, Berger (Collymore 58), Fowler*
Subs not used: Warner, Scales, Ruddock

● *Right:* **Jamie Redknapp in a tug-of-war against Charlton**
● *Below:* **Robbie Fowler is challenged by Blackburn's Graeme Le Saux**

LIVERPOOL 4
CHARLTON ATHLETIC 1

Coca-Cola Cup 3rd Round replay – 13 November 1996 – Att: 20,714

It was back to winning ways for Liverpool in this replay against Charlton at Anfield. Mark Wright and Jamie Redknapp both scored within the first 17 minutes to set the Reds on their way. Shaun Newton pulled one back for the visitors soon afterwards, but Charlton were outclassed for the remainder of the match. Robbie Fowler's two second half goals – a neat flick and a powerful header – put the result beyond doubt.

LIVERPOOL: *James; McAteer, Wright, Ruddock, Matteo, Bjornebye, Thomas, Barnes, Redknapp, McManaman, Fowler*
Scorers: Wright 14, Redknapp 17, Fowler 48, 72
Subs not used: Babb, Collymore, Berger

LEEDS UNITED 0   LIVERPOOL 2

Premier League – 16 November 1996 – Att: 39,981

A full-house at Elland Road saw former Liverpool star Ian Rush line-up for his new club against his old one for the first time. Sadly for Rushie, he found himself on the wrong end of a losing scoreline.

It was a tough encounter with George Graham's Leeds doing their utmost to end a poor spell of results. However, Liverpool's breakthrough came in the 13th minute when Neil Ruddock blasted the ball into the net after the Leeds defence failed to clear a corner.

After that it looked as though the home side might get back into the game. But the Reds held on and, in the last minute of the match, Steve McManaman pounced on a mistake by Nigel Martyn and hammered the loose ball home.

LIVERPOOL: *James; McAteer, Wright, Ruddock, Matteo, Bjornebye, Thomas, Barnes, Redknapp, McManaman, Fowler*
Scorers: Ruddock 13, McManaman 90
Subs not used: Warner, Babb, Collymore, Berger, Kennedy

LIVERPOOL 1   EVERTON 1

Premier League – 20 November 1996 – Att: 40,751

A packed Anfield saw the first Merseyside derby of the season, a game which had been postponed because of heavy rain a month earlier.

Early on Steve McManaman was taken off with a hamstring injury and replaced by Stan Collymore. On the half-hour mark Jamie Redknapp delivered a great cross which Robbie Fowler headed into the top of the Blues' net. In the second period, Everton pressed for an equaliser and it eventually came from a Gary Speed header.

Roy Evans was not overly pleased with his team's performance. 'We lost the plot in the second-half,' he said.

LIVERPOOL: *James; McAteer, Wright, Ruddock, Matteo, Bjornebye, Thomas, Barnes, Redknapp, McManaman (Collymore 17), Fowler*
Scorer: Fowler 30
Subs not used: Warner, Babb, Berger, Kennedy

- *Left:* **Leeds United's Nigel Martyn can only look on as Steve McManaman scores Liverpool's last minute goal**
- *Below:* **Robbie gives Everton the blues**

LIVERPOOL 1   WIMBLEDON 1

Premier League – 23 November 1996 – Att: 38,027

Joe Kinnear's remarkable 'Crazy Gang' were Anfield's next visitors. Liverpool went ahead in the opening minute when the Dons' Dean Blackwell failed to clear a Robbie Fowler flick into the box. Stan Collymore was on hand to quickly snap up the chance.

Both sides went close several times after that and Wimbledon's legendary persistence paid off in the 67th minute when Oyvind Leonhardsen connected with a Marcus Gayle through-ball and fired home the equaliser.

In the final minute the Reds nearly snatched the points when Dons' keeper Neil Sullivan almost allowed a Patrik Berger shot to elude him. The points were shared.

LIVERPOOL: *James; McAteer, Wright, Ruddock, Matteo (Babb 18), Bjornebye, Thomas (Berger 64), Barnes, Redknapp, Collymore, Fowler*
Scorer: Collymore 1
Subs not used: Warner, Kennedy, Jones L

- *Below:* **Neil Ruddock intercepts**
- *Right:* **Arsenal's Martin Keown, Liverpool's Patrik Berger. These cup ties are enough to make your hair stand on end!**

LIVERPOOL 4   ARSENAL 2

Coca-Cola Cup 4th Round – 27 November 1996 – Att: 32,814

Steve McManaman, back from injury, opened Liverpool's account in the 25th minute with an equaliser that cancelled out Ian Wright's earlier penalty for the visitors.

Another penalty, taken by Robbie Fowler in the 39th minute, put Liverpool ahead. Fowler's second, an easy knock-in on 52 minutes from a Jason McAteer cross, stretched the lead.

Arsenal's Steve Bould was given his marching orders by referee Wilkie, but the Gunners came back into the game when Ian Wright scored from yet another penalty kick in the 67th minute.

After that it was Liverpool all the way and the result was sealed at 4-2 by Patrik Berger's blistering 25-yarder which gave John Lukic no chance whatsoever. Liverpool were into the quarter-finals.

LIVERPOOL:
James; McAteer, Wright, Ruddock, Babb, Bjornebye, Thomas, Barnes, McManaman, Berger, Fowler
Scorers: McManaman 25, Fowler 39 (pen), 52, Berger 73
Subs not used: Redknapp, Matteo, Collymore

TOTTENHAM HOTSPUR 0
LIVERPOOL 2

Premier League – 2 December 1996 – Att: 32,898

For the second game in a row, a thoroughly professional Liverpool performance dispensed with a team from north-London.

The opener came virtually on the stroke of half time, when John Barnes set Michael Thomas on route to goal with a great through ball. Mike finished the job by firing across Ian Walker from 10-yards.

Four minutes into the second half, Steve McManaman under-hit a goal attempt. The ball struck a divot and, by a fluke, found its way into Ian Walker's net for Liverpool's second. The victory took Liverpool to second place in the Premiership table.

Afterwards Roy Evans declared himself satisfied with the evening's work - and he joked that 'we bought a portable divot with us!'.

LIVERPOOL: *James; McAteer, Wright, Ruddock, Babb, Bjornebye, Thomas, Barnes, McManaman, Berger, Fowler*
Scorers: Thomas 45, McManaman 49
Subs not used: Warner, Redknapp, Matteo, Kennedy, Jones L

● *Right:* **Wednesday's Pete Atherton keeps tabs on Steve McManaman**
● *Below:* **Michael Thomas opens the scoring at White Hart Lane**

LIVERPOOL 0
SHEFFIELD WEDNESDAY 1

Premier League – 7 December 1996 – Att: 39,507

The only goal came in the 21st minute when Mark Pembridge's shot was diverted in off the post by Guy Whittingham. The Reds almost got back into the game in the 38th minute but Robbie Fowler's effort was magnificently saved by Wednesday 'keeper Kevin Pressman. There were chances at either end after that, but the scoreline remained at 1-0 in the visitors' favour.

It was a disappointing result, to say the least, and the first time that Liverpool had lost at home all season.

LIVERPOOL: *James; McAteer, Wright, Ruddock, Babb (Kennedy 66), Bjornebye, Thomas, Barnes, McManaman, Berger, Fowler*
Subs not used: Warner, Matteo, Cassidy, Jones L

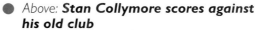

● Above: **Stan Collymore scores against his old club**
● Left: **Stan's a happy man!**

LIVERPOOL: *James; McAteer, Wright, Ruddock, Babb, Bjornebye, Thomas, Barnes, McManaman, Collymore, Fowler*
Scorers: Fowler 1, 28, 77, 85, Bjornebye 45
Subs not used: Warner, Redknapp, Kennedy, Matteo, Jones L

LIVERPOOL 4
NOTTINGHAM FOREST 2

Premier League – 17 December 1996 – Att: 36,126

Another six-goaler came in Liverpool's third consecutive home match. This time it was Stan Collymore's turn to shine – he scored twice against his old club. The first came from a goalkeeping error by Forest's Mark Crossley in the 6th minute. Stan's finished off with a straightforward tap-in. His second came on 63 minutes when he got on the end of a Patrik Berger cross.

In between, Robbie Fowler had headed a Collymore cross past Crossley, and Des Lyttle had headed into his own goal while trying to clear the ball. Forest's replies came from Kevin Campbell and Stuart Pearce.

The result lifted Liverpool back into top spot in the Premiership table.

LIVERPOOL: *James; McAteer, Wright (Matteo 46), Ruddock, Babb, Bjornebye, Thomas, Barnes, McManaman, Collymore, Fowler (Berger 57)*
Scorers: Collymore 6, 63, Fowler 27, Lyttle (og) 51
Subs not used: Warner, Redknapp, Kennedy

LIVERPOOL 5
MIDDLESBROUGH 1

Premier League – 14 December 1996 – Att: 39,491

Liverpool's title challenge got back on track in this match. And what a match it was – especially for Anfield's resident hot-shot Robbie Fowler.

Robbie began a fine afternoon's work by scoring one of the quickest goals of the season, after just 29 seconds. His second strike, on 28 minutes produced his 100th goal for Liverpool. He rounded off a brilliant afternoon by taking his personal tally in the match to four – in the 77th and 85th minutes.

Stig Bjornebye had chipped in with a goal of his own just before half-time. 'Boro's only reply came late in the second half from Jan Aage Fjortoft.

The 5-1 scoreline was an accurate reflection of Liverpool's dominance in the match and had Roy Evan's beaming with pre-Christmas pleasure.

NEWCASTLE UNITED 1
LIVERPOOL 1

Premier League – 23 December 1996 – Att: 36,570

It was off to St James' Park for Liverpool's last match before Christmas. In the 29th minute David James got his hands to a Les Ferdinand header, the ball rebounded off the crossbar and fell to Alan Shearer who knocked it home off his leg.

Liverpool had several chances, and finally broke through for the equaliser just before half-time. Robbie Fowler put away a brilliant cross from Steve McManaman.

As usual when these two teams meet, the game was a real treat and could have gone either way. But this time the points were shared. Afterwards Newcastle boss Kevin Keegan praised his old club and said they looked potential champions.

LIVERPOOL: *James; McAteer, Wright , Ruddock, Babb, Bjornebye, Thomas, Barnes, McManaman, Collymore, Fowler*
Scorer: Fowler 45
Subs not used: Warner, Redknapp, Berger, Matteo, Kennedy, Jones L

- *Right:* **Berger on the ball against Leicester**
- *Below:* **Jason McAteer is tackled by Newcastle's Steve Watson**

LIVERPOOL 1   LEICESTER CITY 1

Premier League – 26 December 1996 – Att: 40,786

At this stage of the season, Martin O'Neill's Leicester City were perhaps the most under-rated side in the Premiership (they would go on to win the Coca-Cola Cup). On this showing they were a real match for Liverpool. Honours were even right up to the 75th minute, when Steve Claridge beat David James with a low, left-sided drive.

Stan Collymore became Anfield's hero when he thundered the ball past Kasey Keller for an 80th minute equaliser. Roy Evans was pleased that his team had displayed its battling qualities to claw back that point.

LIVERPOOL: *James; McAteer, Wright, Ruddock, Babb (Matteo 68), Bjornebye (Kennedy 68), Thomas, Barnes, McManaman, Berger, Collymore*
Scorer: Collymore 80
Subs not used: Warner, Carragher, Jones L

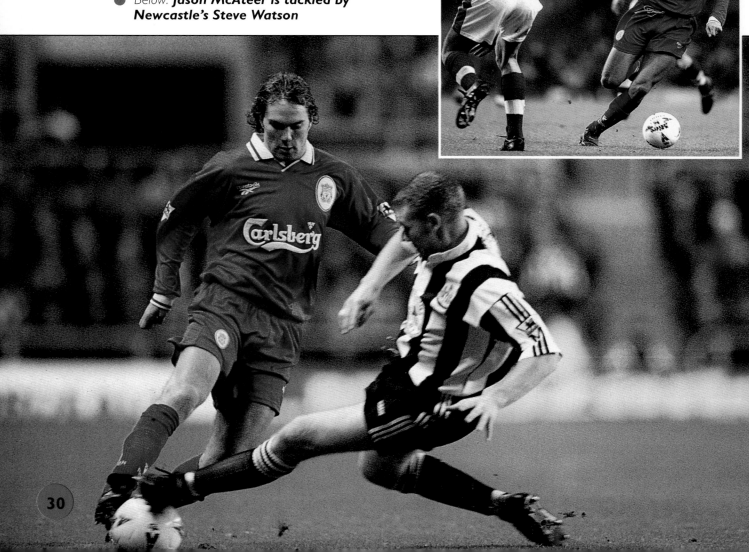

SOUTHAMPTON 0   LIVERPOOL 1

Premier League – 29 December 1996 – Att: 15,222

It was trip to the South Coast for Liverpool's last game of 1996. The Saints piled the pressure throughout, but the Reds stuck to their guns and nothing got through.

The deciding factor was a combination of Dave Beasant's mis-hit clearance from his goalmouth and John Barnes' quick reaction in guiding it into the net from over 40-yards, for the only goal of the game.

The result left Liverpool sitting on top of the Premiership table, five points clear of closest rivals, Arsenal.

LIVERPOOL: *James; McAteer, Wright, Ruddock, Babb, Bjornebye, Thomas, Barnes, McManaman, Collymore (Berger 69), Fowler*
Scorer: Barnes 77
Subs not used: Warner, Kennedy, Matteo, Jones L

- *Main picture:* **John Barnes judges his shot perfectly for his goal at Southampton**
- *Inset:* **Barnsey receives congratulations for his super strike**

MATCH-BY-MATCH - CONTINUES ON PAGE 38

ROBBIE FOWLER
ANFIELD CENTURION!

At Anfield, on 14 December 1996, Robbie Fowler gave himself a couple of early Christmas presents - another matchball and another Man of the Match award to add to his ever increasing collection.

The Toxteth Tornado was well aware that two goals that day in the Premiership clash with Middlesbrough would round off his century of goals for Liverpool FC.

Those two goals would also mean he had reached that target in 165 matches, one less than the record held by his great mentor Ian Rush.

Robbie reached half his target by scoring after just 29 seconds and Rushie's record was broken with his second successful strike. It came in the 28th minute, after a Stan Collymore's shot rebounded to Robbie off the 'Boro goalpost.

The Anfield sureshot returned it right where it belonged for that magical one-hundredth goal of his career.

Everyone at Anfield is now anticipating another speedy century from Liverpool's goal ace!

FACT FILE

Name: Robert Bernard Fowler
Birthdate: 9 April 1975
Birthplace: Liverpool
Height: 5' 8"
Weight: 11st 8lbs
Previous club: None
International: England Full, Youth, 'B' & Under-21

FOWLER'S FIRST TON

Date	Versus	Venue	Competition	Goals
1993-94				
22.9.93	Fulham	(A)	Coca-Cola Cup	1
5.10.93	Fulham	(H)	"	5
16.10.93	Oldham Ath	(H)	Premiership	1
30.10.93	Southampton	(H)	"	3
28.11.93	Aston Villa	(H)	"	1
4.12.93	Sheffield Wed	(A)	"	1
18.12.93	Spurs	(A)	"	2
15.1.94	Oldham Ath	(A)	"	1
13.3.94	Everton	(H)	"	1
23.4.94	West Ham	(A)	"	1
7.5.94	Aston Villa	(A)	"	1
1994-95				
20.8.94	Crystal Palace	(A)	Premiership	1
28.8.94	Arsenal	(H)	"	3
31.8.94	Southampton	(A)	"	1
21.9.94	Burnley	(H)	Coca-Cola Cup	1
5.10.94	Burnley	(A)	"	1
8.10.94	Aston Villa	(H)	Premiership	2
15.10.94	Blackburn R	(A)	"	1
22.10.94	Wimbledon	(H)	"	1
29.10.94	Ipswich Town	(A)	"	2
5.11.94	Nottingham F	(H)	"	1
9.11.94	Chelsea	(H)	"	2
26.11.94	Spurs	(H)	"	1
26.12.94	Leicester City	(A)	"	1
12.12.94	Manchester C	(H)	"	1
31.12.94	Leeds United	(H)	"	1
2.1.95	Norwich City	(H)	"	2
4.2.95	Nottingham F	(A)	"	1
15.2.95	Crystal Palace	(H)	Coca-Cola Cup	1
19.2.95	Wimbledon	(H)	FA Cup	1
4.3.95	Newcastle Utd	(H)	Premiership	1
8.3.95	Crystal Palace	(A)	Coca-Cola Cup	1
11.3.95	Spurs	(H)	FA Cup	1
5.4.95	Southampton	(H)	Premiership	1
12.4.95	Arsenal	(A)	"	1
17.4.95	Leicester City	(H)	"	1
1995-96				
26.8.95	Spurs	(A)	Premiership	1
16.9.95	Blackburn R	(H)	"	1
23.9.95	Bolton W	(H)	"	4
1.10.95	Manchester U	(A)	"	2
4.10.95	Sunderland	(A)	Coca-Cola Cup	1
25.10.95	Manchester C	(H)	"	1
28.10.95	Manchester C	(H)	Premiership	2
18.11.95	Everton	(H)	"	1
17.12.95	Manchester U	(H)	"	2
23.12.95	Arsenal	(H)	"	3
1.1.96	Nottingham F	(H)	"	2
6.1.96	Rochdale	(H)	FA Cup	1
20.1.96	Leeds United	(H)	Premiership	2
31.1.96	Aston Villa	(A)	"	1
11.2.96	QPR	(A)	"	1
18.2.96	Shrewsbury	(A)	FA Cup	1
28.2.96	Charlton Ath	(H)	"	1
3.3.96	Aston Villa	(H)	Premiership	2
16.3.96	Chelsea	(H)	"	1
20.3.96	Leeds United	(H)	FA Cup	1
31.3.96	Aston Villa	(N)	"	2
3.4.96	Newcastle Utd	(H)	Premiership	2
16.4.96	Everton	(A)	"	1
1996-97				
17.8.96	Middlesbrough	(A)	Premiership	1
21.9.96	Chelsea	(H)	"	1
17.10.96	FC Sion	(A)	ECWC	1
23.10.96	Charlton Ath	(A)	Coca-Cola Cup	1
27.10.96	Derby County	(H)	Premiership	2
31.10.96	FC Sion	(H)	ECWC	2
13.11.96	Charlton Ath	(H)	Coca-Cola Cup	2
20.11.96	Everton	(H)	Premiership	1
27.11.96	Arsenal	(H)	Coca-Cola Cup	2
14.12.96	Middlesbrough	(H)	Premiership	2
Total				**100**

FOWLER'S FAVOURITE FOES

The 11 clubs who conceded most goals to Robbie en route to that record breaking century...

Aston Villa	9 goals
Arsenal	7 goals
Fulham	6 goals
Spurs	5 goals
Southampton	5 goals
Bolton Wanderers	4 goals
Chelsea	4 goals
Leeds United	4 goals
Manchester United	4 goals
Manchester City	4 goals
Nottingham Forest	4 goals

● *Below:* **Celebrating another goal**
● *Foot of page:* **Flashback to Wembley 1995**

ARE YOU A SUPER RED?

HERE ARE 20 QUESTIONS TO TEST YOUR KNOWLEDGE OF LIVERPOOL FC...

1 From which club did Bjorn Kvarme join Liverpool?

2 Who did Liverpool beat in the 1995 League Cup final?

3 Who did Roy Evans succeed as Liverpool manager?

4 Against which team did Robbie Fowler score four goals in December 1996?

5 Who captained Liverpool in 1996-97?

6 Which club inflicted Liverpool's worst ever defeat?

7 In which league do Liverpool Reserves compete?

8 How many times have Liverpool won the European Cup?

9 In which town was Steve McManaman born?

10 What is Robbie Fowler's middle name?

11 From which club did Jamie Redknapp join Liverpool?

12 How many times have Liverpool won the FA Cup?

13 Who did Liverpool beat in the 1992 FA Cup final?

14 Which Spice Girl is an avid Liverpool fan?

15 Against which club did Stig Bjornebye score his first goal for Liverpool?

16 Which Football League club did David James use to play for?

17 Who did Liverpool beat in the 1st round of the 1996-97 European Cup-Winners' Cup?

18 Which club did Ian Rush join in 1996?

19 How many times have Liverpool been English champions?

20 Which country does Jason McAteer play for?

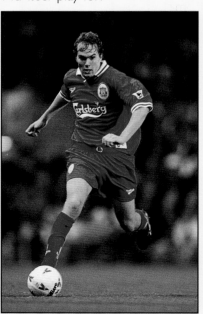

JAMIE REDKNAPP
THE COMEBACK KID

Jamie Redknapp is a wonderful midfield player. He had played just a handful of first team games for Bournemouth – managed by his father Harry Redknapp – when Kenny Dalglish snapped him up for Liverpool for £350,000. That was in January 1991 and Jamie was Kenny's last signing for the club before his shock resignation a few weeks later.

In his first full international, against Colombia in September 1995, it was Jamie's long range shot that caused keeper Rene Huguita to perform the incredible 'scorpion' save that was replayed over and over again.

But Jamie's career was about to be dogged by a string of injuries, all sustained on international duty for England.

In his third appearance, against Switzerland, he tore a hamstring – and eventually made his Liverpool comeback three months later.

Then in the Euro '96 Group A match against Scotland, after coming on as a second half substitute for Stuart Pearce, Jamie broke his ankle and missed much of the first half of Liverpool's '96-97 Premiership campaign.

But he made another comeback, regaining his place in the latter stages and scoring Liverpool's final goal of the competition, against Sheffield Wednesday.

His return to form had brought him back into contention for an international place and he was given his first start under Glenn Hoddle's management in the friendly against South Africa, at Old Trafford in May 1997.

But that international jinx struck again when Jamie was tackled by Phil Masinga.

'It was a tough challenge,' said Jamie. 'But there was no malice involved. I knew immediately I had to come off, but I didn't think it was too serious.'

Imagine his disappointment when an X-ray showed yet another broken bone. 'It was on the same spot as the one I'd sustained the previous summer. I couldn't believe it.'

The injury kept Jamie out of last summer's four-nations tournament in France. And another spell of treatment and physiotherapy meant that 'The Comeback Kid' would have to make yet another Comeback.

FACT FILE
Name: Jamie Frank Redknapp
Birthdate: 25 June 1973
Birthplace: Barton
Height: 6' 0"
Weight: 12st
Previous club: Bournemouth
International: England Full, 'B' & Under-21

● Below: *Jamie with the Coca-Cola Cup in 1995*

ROY IS HUNGRY
FOR SUCCESS

Everyone at Anfield has the feeling that real success – success in the old Liverpool tradition – is only just around the corner. It almost happened in the last two seasons, but the Reds narrowly missed out in the glory stakes.

No one will be more pleased than team manager Roy Evans when success *does* return to Anfield, .

Roy is Liverpool FC through and through. A former England Schoolboy international, he has been involved with the Anfield set-up since leaving school. He graduated to the Reserves team in which he would spend most of his playing career, graduating to

just eleven appearances in the Reds first team in the early-1970s.

When Roy was 25, Bob Paisley recognised his potential as a coach. Taking the great manager's advice, the young man became a member of the renowned 'Boot Room' team, along with Paisley, Ronnie Moran and Joe Fagan – who were all continuing a great Liverpool tradition instigated by Bill Shankly.

Roy managed the Liverpool Reserves team to no less than nine Central League titles in 11 years, helping to groom a whole succession of future first-team stars in the process.

In January 1994 – after

Liverpool had been booted out of the FA Cup by Bristol City – he was named as successor to Graeme Souness as the Reds' first-team manager. This news was met with a measure of scepticism, as few outside the club were even aware of this quietly spoken figure from the Anfield backroom.

But the Liverpool board knew precisely what they were doing in reverting to the old Anfield tradition of promoting from within the club. (Although Souness had been a star player for Liverpool, he had come to the management of the club via Italy and Glasgow Rangers.)

In his tenure in the Liverpool hot-seat, Roy has reshaped the squad to his liking. A number of shrewd transfer deals - Phil Babb, Jason McAteer, Patrik Berger, Bjorn Kvarme etc. - have been balanced by the emergence of several young stars nurtured by the club's excellent youth

- *Above:* **Anxious faces in the dugout**
- *Right:* **The Boss looking cool**

development policy. These include Steve McManaman, Robbie Fowler and Dominic Matteo.

Everyone agrees that Roy Evans has charge of a marvellous squad in a wonderful club with a record that's second-to-none. Surely the missing ingredient - another major trophy or two, to add to Evans' League Cup success of 1995 - cannot be far away.

As if to underline his hunger for success, the modest manager said recently: 'Until I win the Premier League then the name of Roy Evans doesn't deserve to be on the same list as Shankly, Paisley, Fagan and Dalglish. I want to be on it. Not for selfish reasons, but because it would signify that Liverpool were back where they belong.'

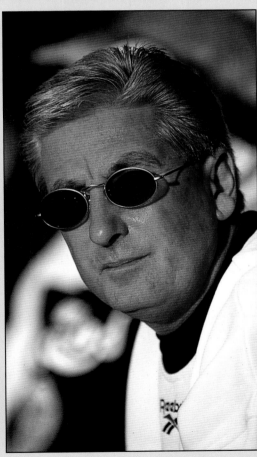

MATCH-BY-MATCH

PART THREE

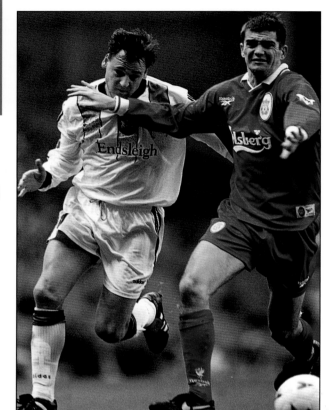

● *Above:* **Dominic Matteo fends off Burnley's Paul Barnes**
● *Below:* **Patrik Berger and Chelsea's Roberto Di Matteo challenge for the ball, while Captain Barnes looks on**

CHELSEA 1   LIVERPOOL 0

Premier League – 1 January 1997 – Att: 28,329

New Year's cheer was definitely not the order of the day for Liverpool after this defeat at Stamford Bridge. The only goal of the game came shortly before half-time. Roberto Di Matteo intercepted a weak pass by Michael Thomas, then charged into the Liverpool area to fire past David James.

Chances to equalise fell to John Barnes and Stan Collymore (twice), but it wasn't to be.

LIVERPOOL: *James; McAteer, Wright (Berger 66), Ruddock (Matteo 34), Babb, Bjornebye, Thomas, Barnes, McManaman, Collymore, Fowler*
Subs not used: Warner, Kennedy, Jones L

LIVERPOOL 1   BURNLEY 0

FA Cup 3rd Round – 4 January 1997 – Att: 33,252

That traditional winter warmer, the 3rd Round of the FA Cup, brought Second Division Burnley to Anfield. And the result was settled after just 12 minutes when Stan Collymore blasted the ball into the corner of Marlon Beresford's net.

Burnley, who had come to Anfield seemingly determined to defend and play for the draw, tried gamely to get back into the match. But Liverpool's resistance was too strong and it saw them safely through to the 4th Round.

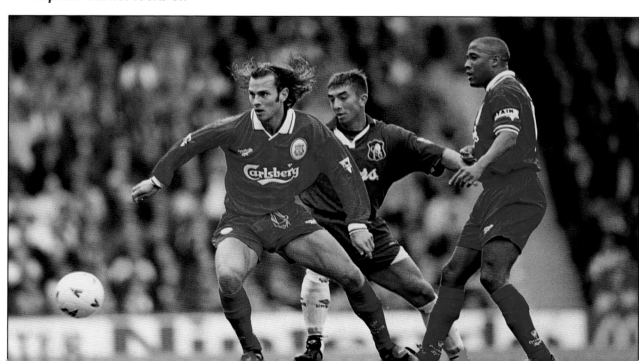

LIVERPOOL: *James; McAteer, Wright, Matteo, Babb, Bjornebye, Thomas, Barnes (Kennedy 67), McManaman, Collymore, Berger*
Scorer: Collymore 12
Subs not used: Warner, Jones L

MIDDLESBROUGH 2
LIVERPOOL 1

Coca-Cola Cup 5th Round – 8 January 1997 – Att: 28,670

A poor performance by Liverpool's standards saw them booted out of the Coca-Cola Cup by an efficient 'Boro side at The Riverside Stadium. The home side were two-up by half-time, through Steve Vickers and ex-Anfield apprentice Craig Hignett.

Liverpool pulled one back through Steve McManaman on 65 minutes and then piled on the pressure as they sought the equaliser. But 'Boro held on for the win and a passage into the Coca-Cola semis.

LIVERPOOL: *James; Jones R (Carragher 74), Wright, Matteo, Babb, Bjornebye (Kennedy 62), McAteer, Thomas, McManaman, Berger, Fowler*
Scorer: McManaman 65
Sub not used: Warner

LIVERPOOL 0
WEST HAM UNITED 0

Premier League – 11 January 1997 – Att: 40,102

The Hammers held out well during Liverpool's onslaught in the opening twenty minutes. John Barnes and Robbie Fowler both rattled the woodwork and Phil Babb had a shot cleared off the line by Mike Hughes.

The match then evened itself out and West Ham got back into it, especially after Babb and Neil Ruddock were both substituted through injury.

In the second period the Hammers almost snatched it, but Mark Reiper's close range header

- Above: **Macca scores against Middlesbrough**
- Below: **Robbie collects the ball**

was brilliantly saved by David James.

In the end a draw seemed a fair result. Meanwhile the results of other matches involving title contenders conspired to keep Liverpool on top of the table.

LIVERPOOL: *James; McAteer, Matteo, Ruddock (Carragher 46), Babb (Collymore 36), Bjornebye, Thomas, Barnes (Kennedy 78), McManaman, Berger, Fowler*
Subs not used: Warner, Jones L

LIVERPOOL 3 ASTON VILLA 0
Premier League – 18 January 1997 – Att: 40,489

In his first start in the Liverpool line-up, young midfielder Jamie Carragher made it a day to remember. He scored the opening goal – a fine header from a Stig Bjornebye corner kick – in the 50th minute.

Another player having a fine Liverpool debut was Norwegian defender Bjorn Kvarme, signed just eight days earlier from Rosenborg. He fitted in well alongside fit-again Mark Wright, and showed just what a great find he was.

Liverpool's second goal came from another header, this time by Stan Collymore in the 58th minute. Robbie Fowler added a third on 63 minutes when he followed up on a Jamie Redknapp shot that had been parried by Villa 'keeper Mark Bosnich.

Roy Evans was delighted with his team's all-round performance, particularly in the second half. And Liverpool still ruled the roost in the Premiership.

LIVERPOOL: *James; McAteer, Kvarme, Wright, Matteo, Bjornebye, Carragher, Redknapp, McManaman, Collymore (Kennedy 75), Fowler*
Scorers: Carragher 50, Collymore 58, Fowler 63
Subs not used: Warner, Harkness, Thompson, Jones L

● **Jamie Redknapp gets away from Villa's Ugo Ehiogu**

CHELSEA 4 LIVERPOOL 2
FA Cup 4th Round – 26 January 1997 – Att: 27,950

Liverpool were two-up at half-time and appeared to be comfortably coasting to a place in the 5th Round. The goals had been expertly taken by Robbie Fowler (from Stig Bjornebye's brilliant build-up) and Stan Collymore's drive under Kevin Hitchcock's body.

The Reds were in control and no-one inside Stamford Bridge or watching on TV could have imagined the Blues turning the game around. Yet, that is precisely what they did.

The Chelsea performance in the second period has to be one of the best of the season. The Liverpool defence seemed to evaporate in the onslaught inspired by Mark Hughes' 50th minute goal. After that it was all Chelsea and further goals from the Italian stars Gianfranco Zola and Gianluca Vialli (who scored twice) completed the remarkable turnaround.

Liverpool were well and truly booted out of the FA Cup – Chelsea would go on to win it.

LIVERPOOL: *James; McAteer, Kvarme, Wright, Matteo, Bjornebye, Barnes, Redknapp, McManaman, Collymore, Fowler (Berger 74)*
Scorers: Fowler 10, Collymore 21
Subs not used: Warner, Carragher

- *Above:* **Chelsea's Steve Clarke tackles Robbie Fowler**
- *Right:* **Macca escapes from Derby's Paul Trollope**

DERBY COUNTY 0   LIVERPOOL 1
Premier League – 1 February 1997 – Att: 18,102

Out of both domestic cup competitions, Liverpool turned their attention once more to the Premiership challenge with a visit to The Baseball Ground.

It was a tough encounter with honours even throughout a first half that produced no goals. Two minutes into the second period, Derby's Darryl Powell was sent-off by referee Peter Jones, for a harsh tackle on Bjorn Kvarme who was later substituted by Michael Thomas.

Liverpool increased the pressure after that and finally broke through for the only goal of the game in the 75th minute when Stan Collymore curled a wonderful left-footed shot beyond the reach of keeper Russell Hoult.

LIVERPOOL: *James; McAteer, Kvarme (Thomas 56),Wright, Babb, Bjornebye, Barnes, Redknapp, McManaman, Collymore, Fowler*
Scorer: Collymore 75
Subs not used: Warner, Jones R, Berger, Kennedy

LIVERPOOL 4   LEEDS UNITED 0

Premier League – 19 February 1997 – Att: 38,957

International action and that enforced absence from the cup competitions meant eighteen days passed before Liverpool's next match. But it was worth the wait!

Leeds United were the victims of a powerful performance by the Anfielders, particularly in the first half. The first goal came from Robbie Fowler in the 22nd minute when the hot-shot striker fired home a brilliant left-sided cross from Stan Collymore. Stan the Man got his name on the score sheet in the 36th minute after collecting a great through ball from John Barnes. Two minutes later Collymore beat Nigel Martyn for the second time after Steve McManaman had beaten two defenders before crossing into Stan's path.

After all that the second half proved an anti-climax. With just three minutes left to play, Leeds conceded a free-kick some 30-yards out. As the defensive wall was sorting itself out Jamie Redknapp blasted the ball into the top corner of Nigel Martyn's net.

Roy Evans was delighted with his team, especially the high standard of their passing.

LIVERPOOL: *James; McAteer, Kvarme, Wright, Matteo, Bjornebye, Barnes, Redknapp, McManaman, Collymore (Berger 79), Fowler (Kennedy 79)*
Scorers: Fowler 22, Collymore 36, 38, Redknapp 87
Subs not used: Warner, Ruddock, Thomas

LIVERPOOL 0 BLACKBURN ROVERS 0

Premier League – 22 February 1997 – Att: 40,747

It just wasn't Robbie Fowler's day!

Twice the young striker's efforts rebounded back into play off the woodwork. And he went very, very close on several other occasions.

In fact, Liverpool created the majority of chances throughout the game, but could not find the net. The Rovers' defence, marshalled by Scottish international Colin Hendry, was in determined mood and ultimately deserved their share of the points.

LIVERPOOL: *James; McAteer, Kvarme, Wright, Matteo, Bjornebye, Barnes, Redknapp, McManaman, Collymore, Fowler*
Subs not used: Warner, Ruddock, Thomas, Berger, Kennedy

● *Opposite page:* **John Barnes is challenged by Blackburn's Graeme Le Saux**

● *Below:* **John Barnes is tackled by Lee Bower of Leeds**

MATCH-BY-MATCH CONTINUES ON PAGE 52

THE DOMINATOR

Dominic Matteo has come a long way since making his Liverpool debut in a 1-1 draw with Manchester City at Maine Road in October 1993. In that game Graeme Souness selected him as a left-sided midfielder. It wasn't Dom's natural position, but he did well enough to be picked a total of eleven times that season.

Late in the 1994-95 he made a handful of appearances, chiefly as a substitute, and he played one game on loan with Sunderland. That was followed by another scattering of Liverpool first team appearances in 1995-96.

It was in 1996-97 that the tall 22-year-old really asserted himself as a central defender. In fact, he was so outstanding in the opening half of the campaign, that stars like Neil Ruddock and John Scales could hardly get a look in (Scales later moved to Tottenham).

Dominic's stunning form also brought him to the attention of England coach Glenn Hoddle who drafted him into the national squad on several occasions.

Born in Scotland, to an English mother and with Italian grandparents on his father's side, Dom was brought up in Southport just a few miles from Liverpool. His footballing talents were obvious and he was quickly snapped up by England before the Scots or Italians could stake their claims!

Dom has been cited as the best Liverpool youth team graduate to emerge since Steve McManaman and Robbie Fowler. He began at the Melwood Centre of Excellence as a 12-year-old and, via a combination of natural talent and sheer persistence, has emerged a decade later at the very top level of the game.

As a lad, Dominic hero-worshipped Liverpool star defender Alan Hansen. These days TV pundit Hansen admires the young man who now dominates the Liverpool defence, just like he used to do!

● *Dom shields the ball from 'Boro's Craig Hignett*

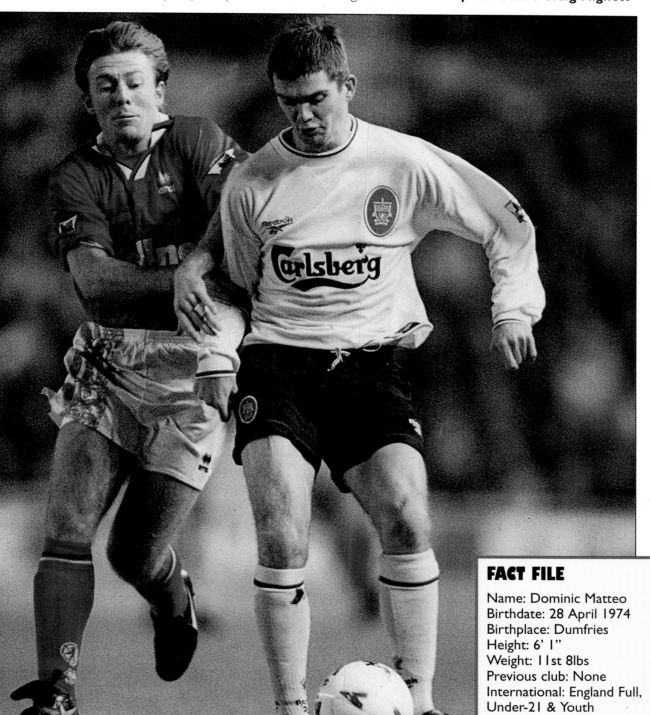

FACT FILE

Name: Dominic Matteo
Birthdate: 28 April 1974
Birthplace: Dumfries
Height: 6' 1"
Weight: 11st 8lbs
Previous club: None
International: England Full, Under-21 & Youth

Stars like Robbie Fowler, Steve McManaman and Dominic Matteo are proof that Liverpool FC has one of the finest youth development schemes in the country.

It is by discovering and nurturing young, talented players that a great club survives. The introduction of players developed at the Melwood complex is every bit as important as those multi-million pound transfers.

Here are just two of the red shirted youngsters awaiting their turn to establish themselves on the first team stage. They are...

STARS OF THE FUTURE

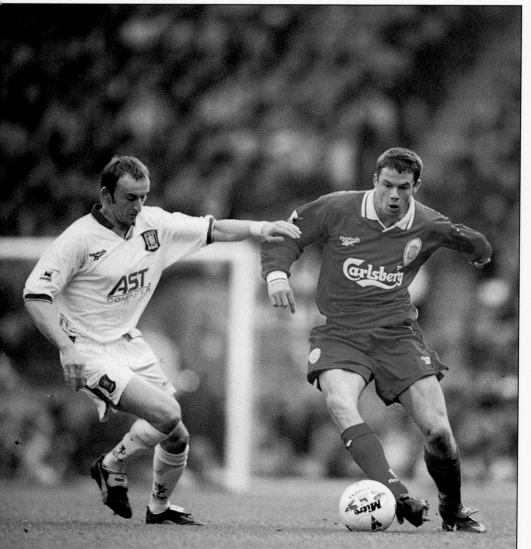

JAMIE CARRAGHER

Defensive midfielder Jamie Carragher had spent a handful of games on the Liverpool bench, when he was called into the starting line-up against Aston Villa on 18 January 1997. And he celebrated by heading the Reds opening goal in a 3-0 victory.

MICHAEL OWEN

Striker Michael Owen made a great impact in the Premiership match against Wimbledon in May 1997. The energy and commitment shown on his second half introduction as a substitute for Patrik Berger gave Liverpool a real boost. And Michael justified Roy Evans' faith by scoring his first Premiership goal in the 74th minute of the match.

The son of former Everton player Terry Owen, Michael confesses that he supported the Blues as a lad. But it was the Reds who recognised his goal-getting skills and his potential when he was an eleven-year-old.

● *Jamie Carragher playing against Aston Villa*

● Top: **Michael Owen on the attack against Sheffield Wednesday**

● Above: **Michael's first Premiership goal, against Wimbledon**

It'll be years, if ever, before anyone comes close to Liverpool's fabulous record. The Anfield Reds are...

ENGLAND'S MOST SUCCESSFUL CLUB

England's most successful football club - 18 times championship winners – was originally formed in 1878 as a club called St Domingo's, a name changed to Everton FC a year later.

By 1880 the club was a member of the Lancashire Association League, playing home games on an open pitch in Stanley Park. Two years later the Lancashire Association decreed that its clubs must play in an enclosed ground. A suitable venue was found in Priory Road, but within another two years the club had moved into a new ground – called Anfield. In 1888 Everton became founder members of the Football League.

Among the club's leading officials at the time was a man named John Houlding, a prosperous brewer, city councillor and a future mayor of Liverpool. Houlding was a very powerful man who virtually ruled the roost at Anfield. This led to him having a number of detractors within the club.

In 1892 a dispute involving the rent of the ground prompted Houlding to part company with the majority of club members and Everton moved on – to a new stadium at Goodison Park on the other side of Stanley Park. This left Houlding with a dilemma on his hands. He had a perfectly good football ground, but no team to play there!

His solution was simple – he formed a new club. At first he attempted to retain the name

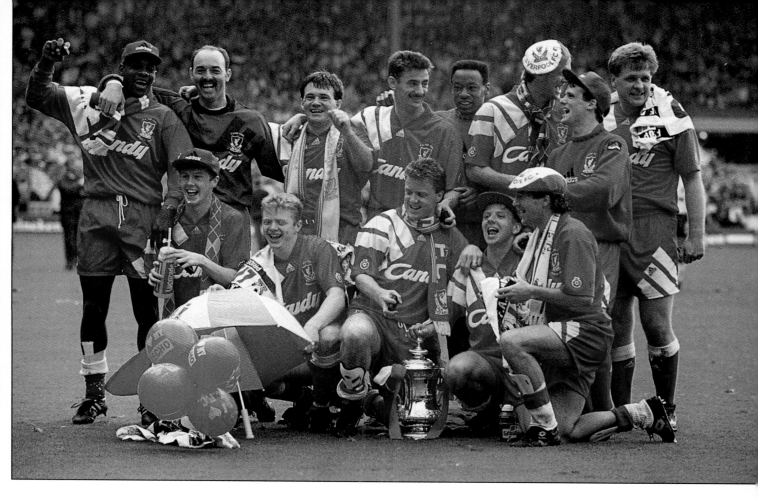

- *Above:* **Liverpool – FA Cup winners 1992**
- *Below:* **Liverpool – League Champions 1987-88**

'Everton', claiming that 'the occupiers of Anfield are the true Everton'. But the FA and the Football League disagreed with him. A new name was needed and, on 15 March 1892, 'Liverpool Association Football Club' was formed and John McKenna appointed as its first manager. Liverpool's first-ever game resulted in a 7-1 victory over Rotherham.

The club applied to join the Second Division of the Football League, but were turned down and joined the Lancashire League instead.

John McKenna built a fine team at Anfield, initially signing no less than thirteen excellent players from his native Scotland. The side was nicknamed 'The Team of Macs' and won the Lancashire League in their very first season. This performance impressed the Football League, and a year after their formation Liverpool FC was admitted to the Second Division.

In Liverpool's very first Football League season – 1893-94 – they became Second

Division champions without losing a single match. To gain promotion to the First Division, they had first to play a 'test match' against Newton Heath (later to become Manchester United) who had finished bottom of Division One. Liverpool won 2-0 and up they went!

At the end of the next season Liverpool were bottom of Division One and once again had to play a 'test match', this time against Division Two champions Bury who won 1-0 to send Liverpool back down again. In 1895-96 they returned to the First Division and were to remain there for the next eight seasons.

In 1898-99 Liverpool were runners-up in the League and FA Cup semi-finalists. In 1900-01 they won their first-ever League Championship, ahead of Sunderland and Notts County.

A dip into the Second Division in 1904-05 was quickly rectified by an instant return to the top flight. This time the Reds stayed for the next 39 seasons, winning the League Championship four times –

The Coca-Cola Cup **Winners 1994/5** The C

● *Above:* **Liverpool – Coca-Cola Cup winners 1995**

1905-06, 1921-22, 1922-23 and 1946-47. They also reached their first FA Cup final, in 1914, against Burnley who won with the only goal of the game.

Thirty-six years later, in 1950, Liverpool reached their second FA Cup final, but lost 2-0 to Arsenal. The remainder of the '50s were to be pretty lean times for the Anfielders. At the end of the 1953-54 season they finished bottom of the First Division and were relegated.

1954-55 saw the club's biggest ever defeat, 1-9 at the hands of Birmingham City at St Andrews. Things improved after that – the Reds came close to promotion four times in the '50s, but remained a Second Division outfit.

Then, in December 1959, a new manager arrived. His name was Bill Shankly and he arrived at Anfield from Huddersfield Town.

'Shanks' would transform Liverpool into one of Europe's top clubs.

He began by *almost* gaining promotion, with a third place spot in 1959-60. In 1961 he released no less than 24

members of the playing staff and then began investing shrewdly in the transfer market. He bought Gordon Milne, a fine midfielder, from Preston; Ron Yeats, a towering defender from Dundee United, and Ian St John an ace goal-getter from Motherwell. His shopping list later included the likes of Peter Thompson from Preston and Willie Stevenson from Rangers. All these players, together with home-grown talents like Roger Hunt, Tommy Lawrence, Jimmy Melia, Gerry Byrne and Ian Callaghan became the backbone of the side.

Bill Shankly's success story began to unfold within three seasons, as Liverpool became Second Division Champions in 1961-62. From then on, only the best would be good enough for anyone connected with the Anfield club; that was Bill Shankly's way.

In 1963-64 the Reds won the League Championship with three games left to play - and Liverpool's glory days were truly under way.

During his fifteen year reign as Liverpool's boss, Shanks brought some great players to the club including Kevin Keegan, John Toshack and Ray Clemence –

and the trophies began to arrive.

When Bill retired in 1974, he had steered his beloved Liverpool to three League Championships,. two FA Cup triumphs and to victory in the UEFA Cup. Following his shock retirement, a few weeks after Liverpool had beaten Newcastle United in the FA Cup final at Wembley, he was succeded by his former assistant Bob Paisley.

Incredibly, Paisley's achievements in the manager's chair were to outshine those of his illustrious predecessor. By the time he retired in 1983 Bob had led the Reds to no less than thirteen major trophies: three European Cup triumphs, six League Championships, three League Cup wins and a UEFA Cup success. Among the many stars of Paisley's side were the great Scot Kenny Dalglish and the ace goalscorer Ian Rush.

Bob Paisley was succeeded in the Anfield hot-seat by another of the legendary Boot Room team, Joe Fagan, who served for the next two years – a relatively short time compared to his predecessors, but a successful one nonetheless. In 1983-84, his first season in charge, Joe led the Reds to glory in three competitions – the League, the League Cup and the European Cup.

Next in line came Kenny Dalglish, one of the finest players ever to pull on a Liverpool shirt. He started his managerial career as player/manager and he did it in real style, winning the League and FA Cup 'double' in his first season (1985-86) and even scoring the goal that clinched the title. He also won two other Championships (1988 and 1990) and a enjoyed further FA Cup success in 1989, before joining Blackburn Rovers in 1991.

Liverpool's next managerial appointment marked the first time in years that the club had not promoted from within. True, Graeme Souness had been a major star and a fine captain at Anfield in his playing days, but he had long since left the club before returning as team boss.

Graeme's reign at Anfield was to be relatively unsuccessful, at least by the high standards set by his predecessors. In his three year spell the only major trophy to come Liverpool's way was the FA Cup of 1992, when the Reds beat Sunderland 2-0 at Wembley.

With the team in something of a slump Graeme Souness left Anfield in 1994, with the unhappy distinction of being the first Liverpool boss to be sacked in 38 years.

He was replaced within two days by Roy Evans, as the club reverted to its policy of appointing managers from inside the club. Evans had been an invaluable member of the Boot Room team since ending his playing career in the days of Bob Paisley.

Roy set about revitalising the team, and his first success came in 1995, when he led the Reds to a

THEY LED THE REDS – LIVERPOOL'S MANAGERS

John McKenna	1892-1896
WE Barclay	1892-1896*
Tom Watson	1896-1915
David Ashworth	1920-1923
Matt McQueen	1923-1928
George Patterson	1928-1936
George Kay	1936-1951
Don Welsh	1951-1956
Phil Taylor	1956-1959
Bill Shankly OBE	1959-1974
Bob Paisley OBE	1974-1983
Joe Fagan	1983-1985
Kenny Dalglish MBE	1985-1991
Graeme Souness	1991-1994
Roy Evans	1994-

*Secretary/Manager

fine Coca-Cola Cup final victory over Bolton Wanderers at Wembley.

Since then Liverpool have always been among the leading challengers to Manchester United's grip on the Premiership title. Last season, 1996-97, the Reds emerged for a while as the favourites to win the championship. But it wasn't to be. They finished a disappointing fourth, but with a place in the 1997-98 UEFA Cup competition

But everyone at Anfield - on and off the pitch – knows the situation will change soon. After all, Liverpool FC is still English football's most successful club!

LIVERPOOL'S ROLL OF HONOUR

LEAGUE CHAMPIONS - 18 TIMES
1900-01, 1905-06, 1921-22, 1922-23, 1946-47, 1963-64, 1965-66, 1972-73, 1975-76, 1976-77, 1978-79, 1979-80, 1981-82, 1982-83, 1983-84, 1985-86, 1987-88, 1989-90

LEAGUE CHAMPIONSHIP RUNNERS-UP – 10 TIMES
1898-99, 1909-10, 1968-69, 1973-74, 1974-75, 1977-78, 1984-85, 1986-87, 1988-89, 1990-91

FA CUP WINNERS – 5 TIMES
1965, 1974, 1986, 1989, 1992

FA CUP RUNNERS-UP – 6 TIMES
1914, 1950, 1971, 1977, 1988, 1996

LEAGUE CUP/MILK CUP/COCA-COLA CUP WINNERS – 5 TIMES
1981, 1982, 1983, 1984, 1995

LEAGUE CUP RUNNERS-UP - TWICE
1978, 1987

SECOND DIVISION CHAMPIONS – 4 TIMES
1893-94, 1895-96, 1904-05, 1961-62

EUROPEAN CUP WINNERS – 4 TIMES
1977, 1978, 1981, 1984

EUROPEAN CUP RUNNERS-UP – ONCE
1985

UEFA CUP WINNERS – TWICE
1973, 1976

EUROPEAN CUP-WINNERS CUP RUNNERS-UP – ONCE
1966

SUPER CUP WINNERS – ONCE
1977

WORLD CLUB CHAMPIONSHIP RUNNERS-UP – ONCE
1981

CHAMPIONSHIP WINNERS

18	LIVERPOOL
11	Manchester United
10	Arsenal
9	Everton
7	Aston Villa
6	Sunderland
4	Newcastle United, Sheffield Wednesday
3	Blackburn Rovers, Huddersfield Town, Leeds United, Wolverhampton Wanderers
2	Burnley, Derby County, Manchester City, Portsmouth, Preston North End, Tottenham Hotspur
1	Chelsea, Ipswich Town, Nottingham Forest, Sheffield United, West Bromwich Albion

MATCH-BY-MATCH

PART FOUR

ASTON VILLA 1   LIVERPOOL 0

Premier League – 2 March 1997 – Att: 39,339

The Reds' title challenge took a hefty blow with this defeat at Villa Park. Yet for 83 minutes the game looked to be heading for a 0-0 draw. Liverpool were enjoying probably their best spell of the match when Villa's Andy Townsend crossed from the left. The ball found Ian Taylor unmarked in front of goal. He finished the job to give the home team all the points.

LIVERPOOL: *James; McAteer, Kvarme, Wright, Matteo, Bjornebye, Barnes, Redknapp, McManaman, Collymore (Berger 54), Fowler*
Subs not used: Warner, Ruddock, Harkness, Kennedy

● **Robbie Fowler and Villa's Mark Draper**

BRANN BERGEN 1   LIVERPOOL 1

European Cup-Winners' Cup Quarter-final 1st leg – 6 March 1997 – Att: 12,700

Liverpool resumed their Euro challenge in Norway, and Robbie Fowler rediscovered his goal-taking instincts. He opened the scoring in the 9th minute with a wonderfully inventive flick that took him round the defence. He then volleyed past keeper Bahus from 10-yards. Brann Bergen would not give up and two minutes into the second period Hasund struck the equaliser with a shot from the edge of the area.

Roy Evans was not displeased with the evening's work and was happy to have an away goal safely in the bag.

LIVERPOOL: *James; Matteo, Ruddock, Harkness, McAteer, Bjornebye, Redknapp, McManaman, Barnes, Berger, Fowler*
Scorer: Fowler 9
Subs not used: Warner, Jones R, Babb, Collymore, Kennedy

LIVERPOOL 4
NEWCASTLE UNITED 3

Premier League – 10 March 1997 – Att: 40,751

In the previous season this fixture had provided arguably the most entertaining match of the entire Premiership programme. The same could be said of it in 1996-97. Once again the stakes were high for both sides – each needed a positive result in order to keep up their respective title challenges.

This time, however, the match began as a really one-sided affair. Liverpool, playing at the top of their game and producing some devastating football, were 3-0 ahead by half time. Steve McManaman, Patrik Berger and Robbie Fowler were the on-target men and it looked for all the world a surefire three-pointer for the home team.

But, as had happened in that dramatic FA Cup tie at Chelsea in January, Liverpool let things slide in the second half. The three-goal margin remained intact until Keith Gillespie scored for the Magpies on 71 minutes after breaking through the Reds'

- *Below inset:* **Patrik Berger celebrates his goal against Newcastle**
- *Below:* **Robbie heads the last minute winner**

defence. Sixteen minutes later Faustino Asprilla got his name on the score sheet when he lofted the ball over David James and into the net.

Nervous anticipation travelled all around Anfield like a Mexican wave. Would Liverpool hold on to that now slender lead? ... Or would Newcastle dig out that equaliser?

The answer came on 88 minutes when Magpies defender Warren Barton blasted a loose ball past David James to make it three goals each.

Now the excitement was almost too much to bear. The result of the previous season's fixture had been settled in Liverpool's favour in the very last minute. Could it happen again?

Answer: Yes. Robbie Fowler popped up in the 90th minute to head home a measured cross from Dominic Matteo. The three points were Liverpool's.

Roy Evans praised his side's first half performance, but could not believe how they had allowed Newcastle to get back into the game in the way that they did.

But for the fans at Anfield and the TV viewers all around the country, Liverpool and Newcastle United had once again provided a Premiership classic. It had end-to-end action, great goals and nail-biting drama – ingredients that go to making the FA Premier League the most fascinating football competition in the world.

LIVERPOOL: *James; Kvarme, Wright, Matteo, McAteer, Bjornebye, Barnes, Redknapp, McManaman, Berger, Fowler*
Scorers: McManaman 28, Berger 31, Fowler 42, 90
Subs not used: Warner, Ruddock, Harkness, Kennedy, Collymore

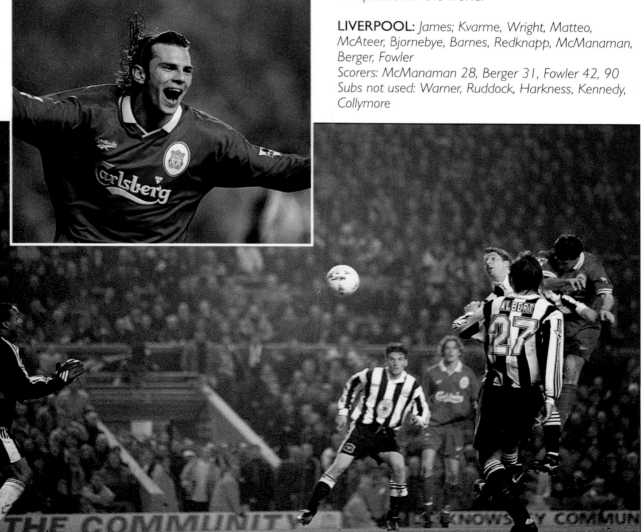

NOTTINGHAM FOREST I
LIVERPOOL I

Premier League - 15 March 1997 - Att: 29,181

Liverpool piled on so much pressure in the opening 30 minutes that Forest's new supremo Dave Bassett later said it was like the Siege of the Alamo!

But only one goal had resulted from that onslaught, scored by Robbie Fowler in the 3rd minute when he chested down a Jason McAteer cross before volleying the ball past Mark Crossley.

Forest got back into the game on the half-hour, when David James dropped the ball and left his goal unguarded during a free-kick situation. Ian Woan was on hand to hit home the loose ball. After that things evened-out and headed for an almost inevitable draw.

LIVERPOOL: *James; Kvarme, Wright, Matteo, McAteer (Harkness 53), Bjornebye, Barnes, Redknapp, McManaman, Berger (Collymore 75), Fowler*
Scorer: Fowler 3
Subs not used: Warner, Ruddock, Kennedy

LIVERPOOL 3   BRANN BERGEN 0

European Cup-Winners' Cup Quarter-Final 2nd leg – 20 March 1997 – Att: 40,326

Liverpool marched into the semi-finals of the European Cup-Winners' Cup with a thoroughly professional performance against the Norwegian side.

The first goal came from the trusty boot of Robbie Fowler, from a penalty awarded when he was brought down by Moen's challenge in the 26th minute.

Stan Collymore provided the Red's second goal after a fine individual run through the Bergen defence. Robbie Fowler wrapped things up in the 77th minute, with a well struck shot from a perfect pass by Stig Bjornebye.

Liverpool had won with a 4-1 aggregate, and the semi-final loomed.

LIVERPOOL: *James; Wright, Harkness, Matteo (Babb 45), McAteer, Bjornebye, Barnes, Redknapp, McManaman, Berger (Collymore 59), Fowler*
Scorer: Fowler 26 (pen), 77, Collymore 82
Subs not used: Warner, Ruddock, Thomas

● *Left:* **Penalty! against Brann Bergen**
● *Below:* **Bjorn Kvarme heads the ball out of defence against Forest**

ARSENAL 1 LIVERPOOL 2

Premier League – 24 March 1997 – Att: 38,068

This superb away victory for Liverpool virtually put paid to Arsenal's title challenge. Stan Collymore scored first after capitalising on a goal-keeping fluff by David Seaman, and stabbing the ball home from about six yards.

The next goal came after one of the most amazing incidents of the entire season. In the 64th minute Robbie Fowler was bearing down on Seaman's goal. The two players fell to the ground. The referee, Mr Ashby, adjudged that Seaman had tripped Fowler and he awarded a penalty to Liverpool.

Then, in a gesture of absolute fair play, Robbie said that he had tripped and therefore it was not a penalty. But the ref's decision stood. Robbie took the penalty kick, which Seaman got to. The ball rebounded into play and Jason McAteer was on hand to score his first ever goal for Liverpool.

Arsenal pulled one back in the 78th minute through Ian Wright, but the game had turned on that extraordinary moment.

The next day's sporting headlines were full of praise for Fowler and he even received a letter of commendation from FIFA the highest authority in the game.

LIVERPOOL: *James; Kvarme, Wright, Harkness, McAteer, Bjornebye, Barnes, Redknapp, McManaman, Collymore, Fowler (Thomas 81)*
Scorer: Collymore 50, McAteer 65
Subs not used: Warner, Ruddock, Kennedy, Berger

- *Above:* **Jason McAteer beats Coventry's Marcus Hall to the ball**
- *Below:* **Stan Collymore is policed by Hughes and Adams of Arsenal**

LIVERPOOL 1   COVENTRY CITY 2

Premier League – 6 April 1997 – Att: 40,079

If Arsenal had slipped up in the previous match, Liverpool were guilty of the same in this game. The Reds scored first, when Robbie Fowler latched on to a John Barnes through-ball in the 53rd minute and volleyed into the top of Steve Ogrizovic's net.

Coventry, down in the relegation zone and desperate for points, came back with Noel Whelan's headed equaliser on 65 minutes. And they won the game in the dying seconds when a David James error allowed Dion Dublin a clear shot at goal after a corner-kick.

LIVERPOOL: *James; Kvarme, Harkness, Matteo, McAteer, Bjornebye (Berger 79), Barnes, Redknapp, McManaman, Collymore, Fowler*
Scorer: Fowler 53
Subs not used: Warner, Ruddock, Kennedy Thomas

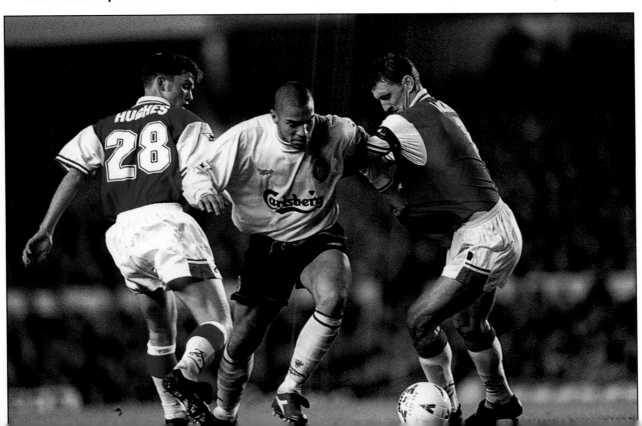

FAIR-PLAY FOWLER!

SUNDERLAND 1 LIVERPOOL 2
Premier League – 13 April 1997 – Att: 21,938

It was good to see Rob Jones back in Premiership action for the Reds. His return coincided with Liverpool's return to winning ways. It was a good game with the home side giving their all in the fight against possible relegation.

The first goal came on 33 minutes when a Stig Bjornebye cross reached Mark Wright who knocked the ball into Robbie Fowler's path. Robbie hit the ball home from close in. Liverpool went two-up two minutes into the second half, thanks to Steve McManaman's clinical finishing of a chance created by John Barnes and Robbie Fowler.

Sunderland's only reply came in the 52nd minute from the head of ex-Anfielder Paul Stewart.

LIVERPOOL: *James; Jones R, Wright, Harkness, Kvarme, Bjornebye, Thomas, Barnes, Redknapp, McManaman, Fowler*
Scorers: Fowler 33, McManaman 47
Subs not used: Warner, Matteo, Kennedy, Berger, Owen

PARIS SAINT-GERMAIN 3 LIVERPOOL 0
European Cup-Winners' Cup Semi-final 1st leg – 10 April 1997 – Att: 35,142

It was poor performance by Liverpool in Paris. David James, in particular, had an uncharacteristically nervy night as goals from Leonardo and Cauet gave PSG just reward for their hard work in the first half.

Liverpool's task in the second-leg was made all the more difficult when Leroy notched PSG's third goal of the game in the 83rd minute.

LIVERPOOL: *James; Matteo, Wright, Harkness, McAteer, Bjornebye, Barnes, Redknapp, McManaman, Collymore (Thomas 46), Fowler*
Subs not used: Warner, Ruddock, Babb, Berger

- Above: **John Barnes in Euro action against PSG**
- Right: **Rob Jones takes a pot shot**
- Below: **Robbie in Roker Park action**

EVERTON 1 LIVERPOOL 1

Premier League – 16 April 1997 – Att: 40,177

A Goodison Park derby match, full of rip-roaring action. Steve McManaman carved out the first goal, by creating space in which Jamie Redknapp was able to score from his pass in the 27th minute. Duncan Ferguson got the Blues' equaliser on 65 minutes, turning and shooting low past David James.

The game was later marred by the double sending-off of Robbie Fowler and Everton's David Unsworth, after they had been involved in a physical confrontation.

LIVERPOOL: *James; R Jones (McAteer 75), Wright, Harkness, Kvarme, Bjornebye, Thomas, Barnes, Redknapp, McManaman, Fowler*
Scorer: Redknapp 27
Subs not used: Warner, Ruddock, Berger, Collymore

LIVERPOOL 1
MANCHESTER UNITED 3

Premier League – 19 April 1997 – Att: 40,892

This was the match in which Manchester United virtually secured their fourth Premiership title in five years. Their convincing victory – with two goals from Gary Pallister and one from Andy Cole – stretched their lead at the top of the table, and left them with the task of simply staying the course.

Liverpool's only reply came from skipper John Barnes. 'Keeper David James once again suffered a

● Above: **Goalmouth action against Manchester United**
● Below: **Jamie Redknapp scores against Everton**

crisis of confidence and had a poor match.

Liverpool now had to concentrate on finishing second in the Premiership. That position would, for the first time, gain entry to the UEFA Champions competition.

LIVERPOOL: *James; Kvarme, Wright, Harkness, McAteer (Collymore 50), Bjornebye, Thomas, Barnes (Berger 67), Redknapp, McManaman, Fowler*
Scorer: Barnes 19
Subs not used: Warner, Jones R, Matteo

LIVERPOOL 2
PARIS SAINT-GERMAIN 0

Premier League – 24 April 1997 – Att: 38,984

More disappointment for Liverpool, despite a truly spirited performance against PSG. Things looked really hopeful after just 12 minutes when Robbie Fowler blasted the ball into the top of the visitors' net.

But the breakthough for the second did not come until the 80th minute. Mark Wright rose to beat PSG keeper Bernard Lama from a corner-kick. Another goal was needed, but it wasn't to be and Liverpool went out of the competition on a 2-3 aggregate.

LIVERPOOL: *James; McAteer, Wright, Ruddock, Bjornebye, Thomas, Redknapp, McManaman, Berger (Kennedy 69), Collymore, Fowler*
Scorer: Fowler 12, Wright 80
Subs not used: Warner, Jones R, Babb, Carragher

LIVERPOOL 2   TOTTENHAM H 1

Premier League – 3 May 1997 – Att: 40,003

This victory over Spurs, in the last Anfield game of the season, moved Liverpool into that all-important second spot in the Premiership table.

The game began badly for the Reds. Darren Anderton's delicate header beat David James and went in off the post in the 5th minute. It took another ten minutes before Liverpool replied, through Stan Collymore who collected Patrik Berger's pass before firing past Ian Walker in the Tottenham goal. Patrik provided the winner in the 43rd minute.

LIVERPOOL: *James; McAteer, Ruddock, Wright, Kvarme, Bjornebye, Thomas, Redknapp, McManaman, Berger, Collymore*
Scorer: Collymore 15, Berger 43
Subs not used: Warner, Barnes, Harkness, Carragher, Owen

WIMBLEDON 2   LIVERPOOL 1

Premier League – 6 May 1997 – Att: 20,016

Liverpool's UEFA Champions' League ambitions took a serious blow with this defeat at Selhurst Park. It was uncharacteristically poor performance from the Reds who went two-down with goals from Jason Euell and Dean Holdsworth.

The only bright spot in the game for the visitors came with the second half introduction of Michael Owen who came on for Patrik Berger. Mike certainly livened thing up, and he scored his first goal for Liverpool when he fired home from a Stig Bjornebye pass in the 74th minute.

LIVERPOOL: *James; Kvarme, McAteer, Ruddock, Wright, Bjornebye, Thomas, Redknapp, McManaman, Berger (Owen 58), Collymore*
Scorer: Owen 74
Subs not used: Warner, Harkness, Barnes, Carragher

SHEFFIELD WEDNESDAY 1
LIVERPOOL 1

Premier League – 11 May 1997 – Att: 39,943

.Wednesday needed to win this match to secure a UEFA Cup place in 1997-98. Liverpool needed a victory to ensure second spot in the Premiership and a place in UEFA Champions' League.

The first goal came in the 73rd minute from Wednesday sub O'Neill Donaldson. The equaliser came from a Jamie Redknapp free kick, following the dismissal of Wednesday's substitute keeper Matt Clarke for handling the ball outside the area.

The draw did neither side any favours. Wednesday missed out on that UEFA Cup berth while Liverpool had to settle for fourth place, behind Newcastle and Arsenal who both notched impressive last day victories.

The Reds only consolation from a long, hard season that had promised so much, was to be a place in the UEFA Cup in 1997-98.

LIVERPOOL: *James; Kvarme (Matteo 46), Wright, Ruddock (Harkness 15), McAteer, Bjornebye, Thomas, Redknapp, McManaman, Collymore (Barnes 46), Owen*
Scorer: Redknapp 83
Subs not used: Warner, Carragher

LIVERPOOL'S PREMIER LEAGUE GOALSCORERS 1996-97

Robbie Fowler	18
Stan Collymore	12
Steve McManaman	7
Patrik Berger	6
John Barnes	4
Jamie Redknapp	3
Michael Thomas	3
Stig-Inge Bjornebye	2
Phil Babb	1
Jamie Carragher	1
Jason McAteer	1
Michael Owen	1
Neil Ruddock	1
Own goals	2
Total	**62**

- *Above:* **Steve McManaman, tackled by Wednesday's Des Walker**
- *Below:* **Michael Owen scores against the Dons**

1996-97 – FA PREMIER LEAGUE – FINAL TABLE

	P	W	D	L	F	A	Pts
1 Man United	38	21	12	5	76	44	75
2 Newcastle Utd	38	19	11	8	73	40	68
3 Arsenal	38	19	11	8	62	32	68
4 LIVERPOOL	38	19	11	8	62	37	68
5 Aston Villa	38	17	10	11	47	34	61
6 Chelsea	38	16	11	11	58	55	59
7 Sheffield Wed	38	14	15	9	50	51	57
8 Wimbledon	38	15	11	12	49	46	56
9 Leicester City	38	12	11	15	46	54	47
10 Tottenham H	38	13	7	18	44	51	46
11 Leeds United	38	11	13	14	28	38	46
12 Derby County	38	11	13	14	45	58	46
13 Blackburn R	38	9	15	14	42	43	42
14 West Ham	38	10	12	16	39	48	42
15 Everton	38	10	12	16	44	57	42
16 Southampton	38	10	11	17	50	56	41
17 Coventry	38	9	14	15	38	54	41
R E L E G A T E D							
18 Sunderland	38	10	10	18	35	53	40
19 Middlesbrough	38	10	12	16	51	60	39*
20 Nottm Forest	38	6	16	16	31	59	34

Middlesbrough had 3 points deducted

LIVERPOOL QUALIFIED FOR THE 1997-98 UEFA CUP

LIVERPOOL REACHED THE 4TH ROUND OF THE 1996-97 FA CUP

LIVERPOOL REACHED THE 5TH ROUND OF THE 1996-97 COCA-COLA CUP

LIVERPOOL REACHED THE SEMI-FINAL OF THE 1996-97 EUROPEAN CUP-WINNERS CUP

STEVE HARKNESS

FACT FILE

Name: Steven Harkness
Birthdate: 27 August 1971
Birthplace: Carlisle
Height: 5' 10"
Weight: 11st 2lbs
Previous clubs: Carlisle United,
Huddersfield Town (loan), Southend
United (loan)
International: England Youth

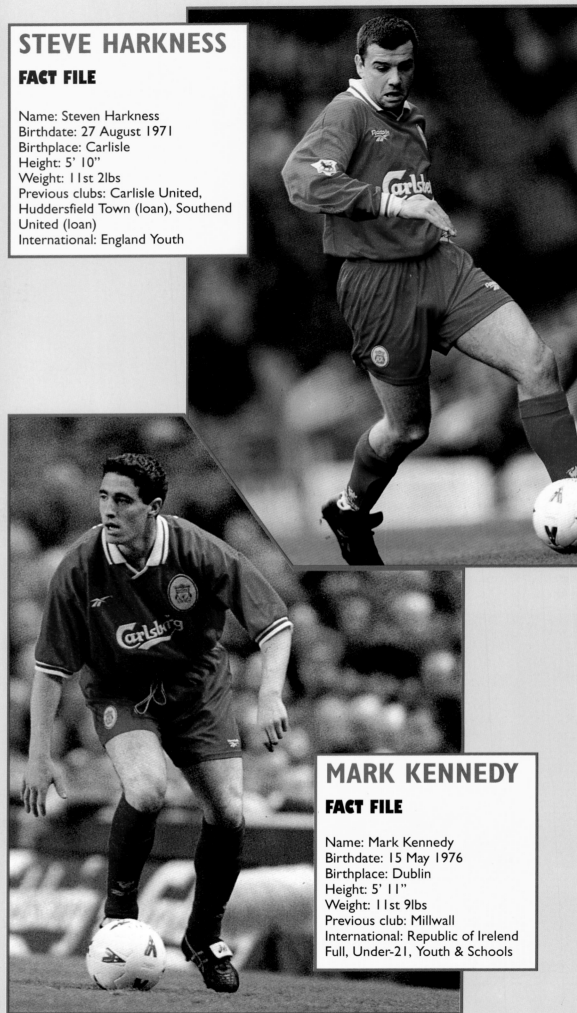

MARK KENNEDY

FACT FILE

Name: Mark Kennedy
Birthdate: 15 May 1976
Birthplace: Dublin
Height: 5' 11"
Weight: 11st 9lbs
Previous club: Millwall
International: Republic of Ireland
Full, Under-21, Youth & Schools

LIVERPOOL FACT FILE

Stadium Address: Anfield Road, Liverpool L4 OTH

Telephone Numbers
Administration — 0151-263 2361
Match Information — 0151-260 9999 (24 hours)
Match Ticket Office — 0151-260 8680 (Office hours only)
Liverworld — 0151-263 1760
Sales & Marketing — 0151-263 9199
Public Relations — 0151 263 2361
LFC Direct Mail Order — 0151-260 1515
Stadium Tours — 0151-260 6677

Chairman: DR Moores
Vice Chairman & Chief Executive: Peter B Robinson
Directors: JT Cross, N White FSCA, TD Smith,
PB Robinson, TW Saunders, KEB Clayton FCA,
DMA Chestnutt FCA, RN Parry BSc FCA
Vice-President: HE Roberts
Secretary: B Morrison
Retail Manager: Kaven Walker
Youth Development Officer: Steve Heighway
Sponsors: Carlsberg

Team Manager: Roy Evans
Assistant Manager: Doug Livermore
Coach: Ronnie Moran
Physio: Mark Leather

Nickname: 'Pool' or 'Reds'
Team Colours: All red
Second Strip: All yellow

Current Ground Capacity: 35,000 (at the start
of the 1997-98 season), 45,000 (by February 1998)
Pitch Size: 110 x 74 yards

Record Attendance: 61,905 v Wolverhampton Wanderers, FA Cup
Fourth Round on 2.2.1952
Record League Victory: 10-1 v Rotherham Town, Second Division
on 18.2.1896
Record Defeat: 1-9 v Birmingham City, Second Division on 11.12.1954
Record Cup Victory: 11-0 v Stromsgodset Drammen, European Cup-
Winners' Cup First Round First Leg on 7.9.1974
Most League Goals in a Season: 106, Second Division on 1895-96
Most Individual League Goals in a Season: 41, by Roger Hunt in 1961-62
Most League Goals in Aggregate: 245, by Roger Hunt between
1959-1969
Most League Appearances: 640, by Ian Callaghan between 1960-1978
Record Transfer Out: Stan Collymore to Aston Villa for £7 million
Record Transfer In: Stan Collymore from Nottingham Forest
for £8.5 million

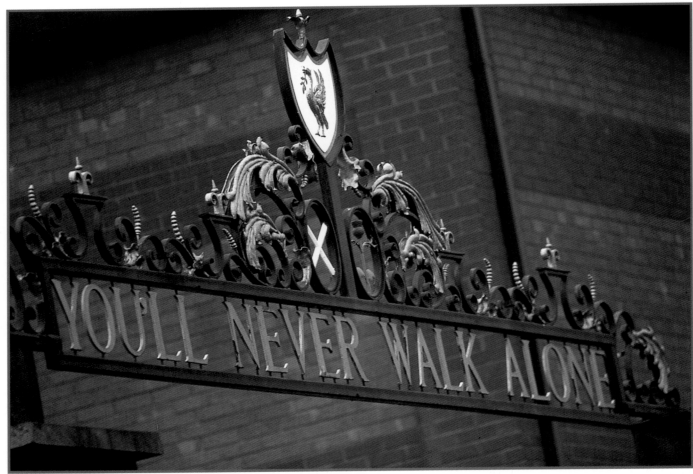